RELAX NOW

RELAX NOW

Removing Stress from your Life

by Sheila Hayward

Sterling Publishing Co., Inc.
New York
A Sterling/Silver Book

A QUARTO BOOK

Library of Congress Cataloging-in-Publication-Data is available upon request.

10 9 8 7 6 5 4 3 2 1

Published by Sterling Publishing Company, Inc.
387 Park Avenue South, New York, N. Y. 10016

Copyright © 1998 Quarto Inc.

Distributed in Canada by Sterling Publishing
c/o Canadian Manda Group, One Atlantic Avenue, Suite 105, Toronto, Ontario, Canada M6K 3EK

Printed and bound in China

ISBN 0-8069-6309-3

This book was designed and produced by:
Quarto Publishing plc
The Old Brewery
6 Blundell Street
London N7 9BH

Senior project editor **Gerrie Purcell**
Text editors **Diana Craig and Hilary Sagar**
Indexer **Dorothy Frame**
Designer **Simon Wilder**
Photographers **Richard Gleed and Paul Forrester**
Illustrator **Stuart Robertson / The Ink Shed**
Picture researcher **Gill Metcalf**
Senior art editor **Penny Cobb**
Art director **Moira Clinch**
Publisher **Marion Hasson**

Typeset in Great Britain by Central Southern Typesetters, Eastbourne
Manufactured in Hong Kong by Regent Publishing Services Ltd.
Printed in China by Leefung-Asco Printers Ltd

C O N

TENTS

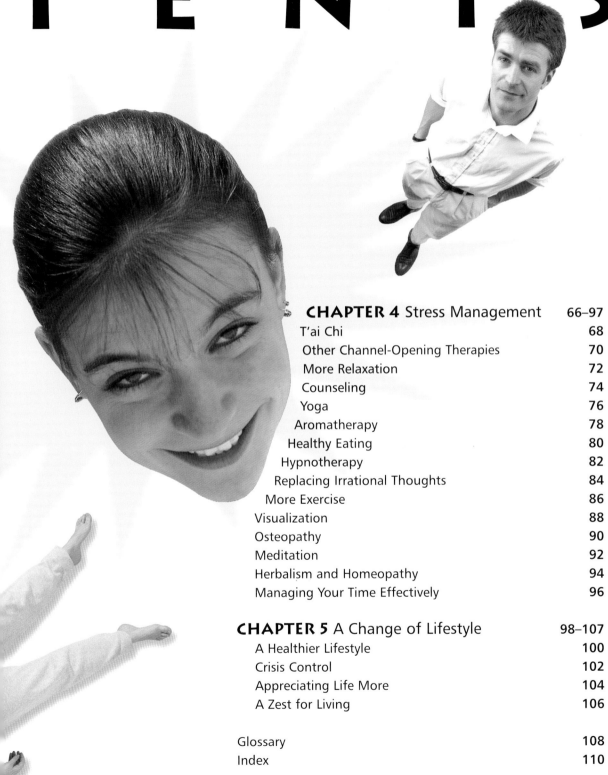

INTRODUCTION

Is stress a "modern problem"? Probably not; early man may have suffered stress because he could not find enough to eat, or was threatened by wild animals or hostile neighbors. Our stressors are different nowadays, but this does not mean that they are less real—or any less threatening.

We may have problems at work: too much work, or work that is too difficult. Conversely, our work may be too easy and therefore boring, or we may have too little work, which raises worries about possible redundancy. Concerns about the environment, traffic, pollution, feelings of helplessness, and inadequacy beset most people at some time or another; concerns about the society in which we live are natural. Modern stresses and strains, however, can take over and rule your life, if you let them. Take steps to make sure this does not happen—take control of your own life.

We are all different individuals, so what upsets, angers, or causes stress or anxiety to one person does not necessarily have the same effect on someone else. When you voice your problems, it does not help to be told, "Oh, you don't want to worry about *that*, that's nothing! Now if you had my problems…"

Because anxieties and stress are so personal, it is up to each of us to find our own solutions to our problems—but how? This is where this book can help; it outlines a range of solutions for you to try (some are instantaneous and some need practice, as not everything which is beneficial is achieved instantly)! The first chapter describes some "instant solutions" for you to try, techniques which can be used immediately without the need for understanding, rather like taking a painkiller for a headache. When your headache is better, you may want to analyze what caused it, and it's the same with stress— when you can think rationally, you'll be able to read through the book and work out a long-term strategy so that you can manage

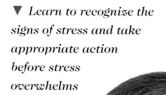

▼ *Learn to recognize the signs of stress and take appropriate action before stress overwhelms you.*

your stressful encounters in the future, without feeling that the world is crashing about you.

This book will not "cure" stress; stress is always going to be with us. What the book aims to do is to show you how to manage your stress, and how to adapt your lifestyle if necessary so that you become more resilient and problems bounce off you, rather than leaving dents in you. The book, of course, cannot do this by itself; it needs you to read it, to absorb what it says, to try the techniques advocated, and practice those which suit you, those which you can incorporate easily into your lifestyle. However, you need to be realistic about the changes you want to make. Sweeping changes may sound attractive, but small, regular steps often achieve more, because you can adhere to them more consistently.

▲ *Stress is not solely a modern problem—early man's problems were finding enough to eat; perhaps his paintings helped resolve his stress.*

WHERE DO THESE TECHNIQUES COME FROM?

I first became interested in stress about 25 years ago, when I was young and—I thought—indestructible. I refused to acknowledge that I was over-working, anxious, and worried, and tried to maintain a lifestyle which I

◀ *When you are feeling stressed, transport yourself, physically or mentally, to a favorite relaxing place.*

can now see was impossible. I stayed sane but my physical health broke down, which made me realize that stress affects the body as much as the mind, and that I should change my lifestyle. Over the years I have researched stress extensively, carried out surveys into occupational stress, and run stress management courses, which I have had evaluated by the participants. The techniques in this book are mainly derived from this experience. A few others are techniques which have been advocated by friends and clients, but which I myself do not use—but, as I said earlier, we are all different, and I am the first to acknowledge that some things which do not appeal to me may produce excellent results for others. So I will tell you about those, too, and you can try them for yourself.

◀ *Any form of exercise releases beneficial chemicals in the body, gives feelings of well-being and promotes physical health.*

WHAT WILL THE
TECHNIQUES DO FOR ME?

Some will make an instant difference to your state of mind and feelings of physical and mental wellbeing. Others will take a little longer to have effect, but their effects will be longer-lasting. Ultimately, if you follow the advice in this book, you could reasonably expect to:

✷ cope better with anxieties

✷ reduce negative thoughts

✷ become emotionally stronger

✷ improve your problem-solving abilities

✷ become calmer and more tolerant

✷ increase your physical fitness

✷ develop a more positive attitude about your life

✷ find more zest for living

Is it worth a try? You have nothing to lose, and everything to gain. But remember, you have to take ownership, not only of your stress, but of your solutions, too. In writing this book, I can show you the way, but I can't make you use the techniques; that is up to you. However, success breeds success, and as you begin to feel better and stronger and more positive, it will encourage you to continue.

▼ *Taking control of your life reduces anxieties and produces a more positive outlook.*

AND FINALLY ...

This book is written for the people counselors never see in stress management classes: those who are too busy to come; those who are so stressed they believe it is normal; those who wish to hold onto their stress and make it a part of their personality—until they reach critical breaking point. As they have no strategies to put into place to save themselves, they can now reach for this book!

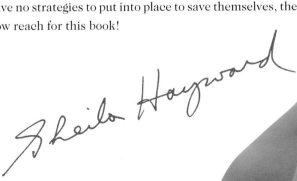

CHAPTER 1

INSTANT SOLUTIONS

In our lifetime each of us experiences different levels of stress, sometimes changing daily. Occasionally we all reach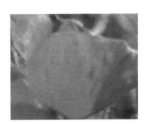

what we feel is breaking point—a crisis in our lives, such as sudden loss of a job, bereavement, physical or emotional trauma. These need immediate relief, and if there is no one standing by to help, the first chapter of this book can provide some instant solutions—"quick-fix" techniques to make things seem bearable again. It is hoped that when your crisis is over, you will feel strong

 enough to explore further into this book and find the origins of what helped you through. Finally, do try to get help in a crisis.

BREATHING TECHNIQUES

Before you begin these breathing exercises, it is important to realize that it's the *in-breath* (breathing in) that creates tension within the body, while the *out-breath* (breathing out) releases that tension. "Concentrate on the *out-breath*" is the best advice.

DEEPENING YOUR BREATHING

Many people use only the top part of their lungs when they are breathing, so that air is not drawn into the lower lobes. Place your hands lightly on the diaphragm area (at the bottom of the rib-cage, where the ribs part). Now breathe in, pushing against the hands, to the full expansion of the lungs. To begin with, you may find this easier if you are lying on the floor, with your knees bent. Now slowly expel all the air in a long, slow out-breath.

REGULATING YOUR BREATHING

This technique can be carried out anywhere, at any time. Even in a crowded place, others are likely to be unaware that you are using a breathing technique. Breathe in, counting to two (one-two, fairly slowly). Hold that breath, and count to two again. Now breathe out, counting to four, concentrating fully on the out-breath. It may help you to concentrate if you visualize the air leaving the nostrils on the out-breath. Repeat this technique several times, then try it with your eyes closed.

You may find it suits you better to increase the count, to three or even four, on the in-breath, but remember to keep the *holding* count equal to the in-breath; the count for the out-breath should be twice as long as the in-breath. Counts may be: Two-two-four; three-three-six; or four-four-eight. Regulating the breathing in this way releases tension through the out-breath.

▲ ▶ *Place your hand lightly on your diaphragm. You should feel it move as you breathe, if you are making full use of your lungs.*

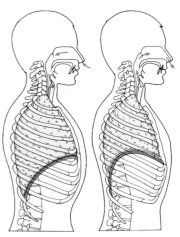

Breathing in   Breathing out

SLOWING THE BREATHING

Lie on your back on the floor using a cushion or towel to protect your head and neck. You may feel more comfortable if you have your knees bent, or you may prefer to lie flat; either will do. As you breathe in, raise your arms over your head, bending them gently at the elbow, and lower them to rest on the floor, level with or above your head. Leave them there as you breathe out. On the next in-breath, bring them gently and slowly back to your side. Leave them by your side as you breathe out. Now repeat the whole process as you breathe in again, raising or lowering the arms on the in-breath, keeping them still on the out-breath.

Try this with your eyes closed. Note what is happening to your breathing, after several minutes. Yes, it is slower than you ever thought possible. A slow breath is a calm breath.

1 *To slow the breath, lie on the floor, with your legs bent or straight, and raise your arms into the air as you breathe in.*

2 *Lower your arms to the floor, bending them at the elbow. Keep this position and breathe out slowly.*

3 *Breathe in again as you slowly lower your arms to your sides. Keep this position as you breathe out.*

QUICK RELAXATION

The art of relaxation needs practice, like all skills. You will achieve some benefit from your first attempts, but the more you use the techniques, the more effective they will be. The two techniques described below are for use when you only have a few minutes to spare, but desperately need to "switch off," for example between one business meeting and the next.

TWO-MINUTE TECHNIQUE

For this technique, you need an upright chair with arms, which is the right height so that you can sit with your feet flat on the floor. Fortunately many office chairs nowadays are adjustable for height and back-position. Sit well back in the chair, so that your back is supported. Your feet should be flat on the floor and your ankles should be directly under the knees, which are bent at right angles (see left). If your chair has arms then rest your arms on the arms of the chair; these should be at the right height so that your shoulders are not forced upward, as this induces tension in the body. If your chair has not got arms or the arms are too high, rest your hands on your thighs or knees instead. The head, the heaviest part of the body for its size, needs to be balanced nicely on top. Drop your shoulders, close your eyes, and gently give a little "nod" of the head, to relax the all-important neck muscles, where tension is so often stored. Now that all the weight of your body is being taken by the skeleton, you do not need to tense your muscles to hold yourself erect. Give those muscles "permission" to relax! Think about your breathing, think about the out-breath, that takes tension out of the body. Count "one" on every out-breath, or if you prefer, say to yourself "calm" or "relax" on every out-breath. Do this for two or three minutes, and you are ready to face the world again!

◀ *The muscles take minimal strain in this seated relaxation position.*

QUICK VISUALIZATION

You may be feeling stressed and even mentally or physically exhausted, but you still have much to do; for example, you may have been rushing around shopping, and now you have to hurry and get ready to go out for dinner—or even, cook the dinner yourself! If you just battle on, you know you will become more tired and irritable, get more stressed, make mistakes, or be downright unpleasant to people. What can you do? Take two or three minutes to use the following technique.

Remove your shoes, lie against a wall with your buttocks as close as possible to the wall and your legs up the wall. Close your eyes and visualize all the tiredness draining away from you, draining from your feet, down your legs, through your body, and running out of the top of your head, leaving your mind clear and untroubled, and your body rested and refreshed. Do this for two or three minutes, and you will soon be ready to "go" again!

▶ *Tired and aching after a long day? This position will help you to relax and unwind in just a few minutes.*

SLOW RELAXATION

The aim of relaxation is to relax the body totally so that there is no tension in it, and to extend this relaxed state to the mind. The benefits of total relaxation are an enhanced feeling of peace and wellbeing, and complete invigoration.

TEN-MINUTE TECHNIQUE

As with most techniques, there is a right and wrong way of going about it. If you were asked to lie on your back on the floor, and you complied, it would be a fair guess that you could slide one or both hands in the space between the floor and the small of your back. So your back is *not* on the floor, and those all-important lumbar muscles, which work so hard keeping you upright all day, and protest in the form of backache, have not been given permission to switch off and relax. Let's do it the right way.

1 Sit on the floor, with your feet apart and your knees slightly bent. Your feet should be about 6–12 inches (15–30cm) apart. Lean forward over the knees, with your arms hanging over toward your toes. Stay like this for a minute, to allow those lumbar muscles time to stretch out. Give them permission to relax and go "off duty." **2** Take your hands back to hip level and gently begin to unpeel yourself back onto the floor, taking your weight first on the hands **3** then on the forearms, then elbows **4** until finally you are lying flat on the floor. Do not ask your back muscles to take the strain at any of these stages—they are off duty; take your weight on your arms. Allow your feet to "fall" outward; this relaxes the hip joints. Now, just check to see whether your back is flatter to the floor; you may find you can still slide a few fingers beneath the small of the back and the floor, but not like last time. Each time you do this, your back will relax more and more toward the ground.

1

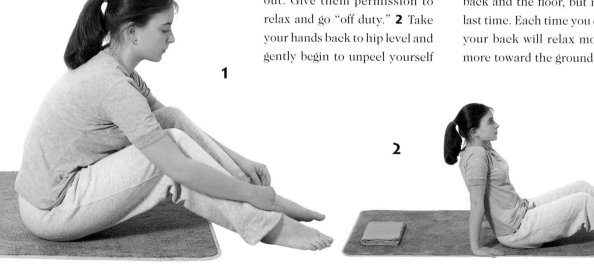

2

▲ *Your favorite relaxing place could be anywhere you choose—a country scene or a paradise island.*

Imagine someone has taken hold of your wrists and is pulling your arms gently away from the sides of your body. Turn the palms of your hands up to the ceiling; this relaxes the shoulder joints and muscles.

Stretch the back of the neck along the floor. Gently allow your eyes to close (wearers of contact lenses may need to remove lenses before doing this exercise).

RELAXATION SCRIPTS

Using the following scripts, say the words to yourself (it is not necessary to be word-perfect—an approximation will be adequate).

✶ Listen for any sounds outside the room. Don't judge them, let them go.

✶ Listen for any sounds inside the room. Don't judge them, let them go.

✶ Listen for any sounds inside your own body. Don't judge them, let them go.

✶ Be aware of the breath entering and leaving the nostrils; be aware of the *out-breath*; count "one" on the out-breath, or if you prefer, say "calm" or "relax" or any other word of your choice which does not evoke an emotional response.

Do this for as long as you wish, remembering to say your chosen word on the out-breath. Do not let your thoughts wander off.

NOW IMAGINE YOUR FAVORITE RELAXING PLACE …
a place where you have felt comfortable and relaxed in the past. Imagine yourself there.

✶ Visualize the colors there … Concentrate on one of the colors … perhaps your favorite color.

✶ Listen for any sounds … in your favorite relaxing place.

✶ Smell any aromas … in your favorite relaxing place.

✶ Touch any object there.

ENDING THE RELAXATION
Tell yourself: I am now going to count to three; when I do, I shall open my eyes and sit up and feel completely refreshed.

One … two … three …
Well done!

3

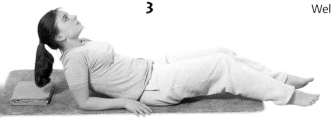

4

EXERCISE

Exercise is a wonderful stressbuster, for two good reasons. First, it removes you, physically, from the situation that is causing the stress, as it is usually not practical to exercise on the spot! Second, during exercise you use up all the "stress chemicals" which are circulating in your body, and start to manufacture beneficial chemicals, such as endorphins.

CHOOSING AN EXERCISE

Any form of exercise will do. How fit you are already, your age, and the immediate availability of some forms of exercise and suitable clothing are some of the constraints you need to consider. If you have never played squash before, or gone jogging, it is recommended to check first with your doctor before embarking on strenuous exercise, so as an "immediate solution" these may be available to only a few people. However, types of exercise that anyone can do instantly include:

Walking For good oxygenation, walking should be done at a good brisk pace, preferably in open countryside, but a town park will do. Failing the availability of that, a brisk walk round your block, main street, or even the shopping mall, is better than nothing! Make it 20 minutes, resist the temptation to get side-tracked into shops, and see how much

better you feel when you return. If possible, follow a route that takes in a slight hill, just enough to make you "puff" slightly without getting exhausted, or increase the speed of your walking for a stretch, to make

yourself out of breath. The extra oxygen you will then take in will be of benefit to you.

Sports You may not instantly find enough people to play a team game, but you may find a partner

◀ *Riding a horse is more than just exercise — you can enjoy the countryside and reaffirm your own relationship with nature and your horse.*

for tennis or golf at short notice. Alternatively, there are sports which can be practiced alone, at very short notice: horseriding, skiing (no snow? where's your nearest dry-ski slope?), ice skating, rollerblading, or roller-skating.

Swimming This exercises all the muscles without putting strain on joints, and is therefore an excellent form of exercise for anyone who is overweight. Can't swim? Join a class specially for adult learners, or buy some armbands and teach yourself. Even just splashing about in the shallow end is stress-reducing. Freud would have suggested that the water was taking us back to the time we spent floating in the womb, which was probably the most stress-free time in our lives!

Gym exercise If you don't already belong to a gym, now may be the time to join. Good fitness centers will assess your fitness and recommend exercises for you specifically. It doesn't cost the earth, and you then have a

◀ Swimming is an excellent form of exercise for all ages; the muscles are given a good workout but the joints take no strain.

program you can refer to in the future. In fact, the mere process of assessment is stress-reducing in itself, because you get the feeling that someone really cares about you. Aerobics classes are another option, but if you feel you are not fit enough for aerobics, try aquarobics; the water softens the impact on the body while still producing the beneficial effects of exercise, as well as offering the therapeutic effects of water.

Dancing Choose your own type of dancing. Wonderful exercise, incredibly liberating! Can't do it? Don't worry, neither can most of the other people on the dance floor! If you can't find any dancing available immediately, put the radio or a CD on, and dance alone. It's still good exercise, you can practice new steps, and if you fall over, no one else will see!

MASSAGE

There are reputable massage parlors in most towns and cities, and a large number of well-trained individuals who work from home or health centers dedicated to alternative therapies. Some organizations employ masseurs on company premises, for use by employees; if your company does not, maybe you should try suggesting it sometime.

TYPES OF MASSAGE

There are many types of massage. Swedish massage is possibly the best known; it is a systematic routine of basic strokes, involving work over the whole body. Other systems have originated in the East, and some incorporate both Eastern and Western techniques. In some cultures, body massage is an accepted way of life, promoting physical and mental wellbeing.

If you have recently suffered injury, such as tendon damage, or if you suffer from high blood pressure, thrombosis, diabetes, osteoporosis or kidney problems, then possibly massage should only be undertaken with medical advice. The gentler forms of massage may be appropriate, but always inform your masseur of any health problems.

Body massage A full-body massage removes the tension from all the muscles and joints

▲ *Shoulder Massage*
Squeeze and knead knotted muscles in the shoulders and at the base of the neck to relieve tension.

of the body, inducing a feeling of calm. Some masseurs use aromatherapy oils to enhance the calming effect.

Head and shoulders massage
If you cannot spare the time for a full-body massage, ask for just a head and neck treatment. Much of the tension caused by stress is held in the neck and

▲ *Head Massage*
Massage the knot of muscles at the base of the skull, and move up over the scalp to relieve tension headaches.

scalp muscles, and this is why headaches often seem to start in the back of the neck and spread upward over the scalp. A massage for the head and neck (as shown above) relaxes those muscles.

Self-massage No time to go out for even a head and neck massage? Then self-massage may be the answer.

▲ *SELF-MASSAGE*
Using your fingertips, gently massage around the bony ridge encircling the eyes.

We have already identified the neck as one of the places most susceptible to muscular tension. Place the first two fingers of each hand on the back of your neck. Do you feel a little knot of muscles here? Gently massage both sides of the neck with an outward, circular motion. Try closing your eyes, as this helps tension dissolve. Do this for several minutes and you will feel the knot of muscles relax.

Another place which benefits from gentle self-massage is around the eyes. Place the tips of your fingers on the eyebrows, near the nose. Gently sweep the fingers outward to the temples, around the bony ridge of the eye

sockets (see left), and up each side of the nose to the point where you first started. Do this continuously, in a smooth, circular motion, until you have swept the tension away.

The shoulders, too, carry a great deal of muscular tension. Place your hands on your shoulders, where the neck and shoulders join. Are there tense knots of muscles here? Squeeze and massage these knots until they release. If you can find a friend or loved one who will do this for you, so much the better.

Cupping the eyes Finally, here is something akin to massage that is very comforting. Rub the palms of your hands together very briskly for a minute or so, until they feel really warm, then gently place them over

your closed eyes. Feel the warmth of your hands and their energy seeping into the area around your eyes. Open your eyes behind your palms, looking into their warmth, then gently slide your hands away from your eyes, outward over the ridges of the eyebrows.

▼ *Gently place your warmed hands over your eyes—do not rub or squeeze, simply enjoy the warmth.*

REFLEXOLOGY

Reflexology has its roots in the Chinese "channel-opening" therapies. It is a bodywork massage technique that consists of stroking or applying pressure to one part of the body in order to effect changes in another part of the body. Types of reflexology include hand, body, and foot reflexology and zone therapy.

FOOT REFLEXOLOGY

Perhaps the most widely used and easily accessible way to practice reflexology on yourself is foot reflexology. The basic idea is that the foot represents a map of the whole body. The big toe represents the head and neck and, following in a line down the inside edge of the foot represents the spinal column. Other areas of the body are represented by other parts of the foot.

The full benefit of foot reflexology is not always apparent the first time you use it. You will feel some benefit and stress relief, but, as it is a therapy, you will become aware of its full potential the more you use it.

The technique Make sure your nails are short, and, if you have any injuries or abrasions on the foot, do not massage over these. Treat both feet in the same way.

Apply a spot of body lotion, then rub and knead the foot.

Massage the foot in small, circular movements. When working the toes, rub and gently pull each one separately. Press the thumbs or pads of the fingers into any part that needs relieving. It is important to press firmly enough not to tickle.

The reflexology points

Many areas of the body are associated with stress, but particularly the head, neck, and spinal column. For stress relief, those points on the "foot map" that relate to these are the

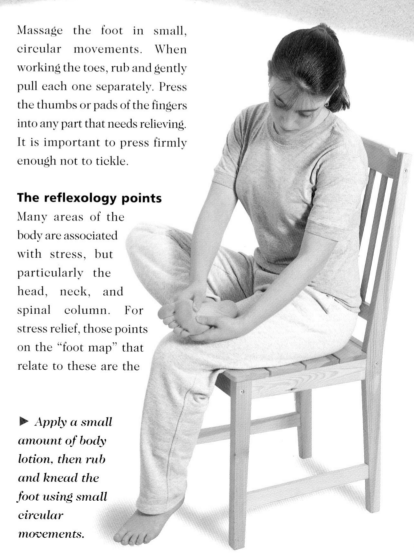

▶ *Apply a small amount of body lotion, then rub and knead the foot using small circular movements.*

big toe
and the inner
edge of the foot, and these
should be given extra attention.
If you feel that your stress is
concentrated mainly in your
head, perhaps causing a headache, massage, squeeze, and pull
the big toe. If your back seems
to be taking the strain, you have
backache, or your posture has
slumped, then the inner edge of
the foot needs firm massage,
pressing and kneading from the
toe end of the foot toward the
heel, on both sides of the foot.

If you regard the solar plexus
(stomach) area as the center of
your being, that area suffers
under stress; its corresponding
area in the foot is on the ball of
the foot. If you feel along the ball,
from beneath the big toe, there
is a V-shaped indentation which
relates to the solar plexus.

Pressure
applied here with
the pad of the thumb will be
stress-reducing.

Going barefoot Walking with
no shoes on provides a natural
massage for the foot; but,
unfortunately we do not do this
often enough each day. Take
every opportunity you can to go
barefoot. Even when you are
sitting at your desk, it may be
possible to remove your shoes.
A piece of round dowel-rod, or a
wooden foot-massager, can be
used discreetly under your desk,
or when sitting at home watching
television.

◀ *Make or buy a
foot-massager; it can
be used any time you
are seated—even at
work under the desk.*

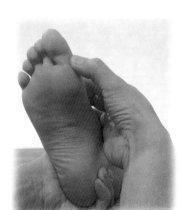

▲ *Massage the big toe and
its "neck," which represent
the head and neck, to reduce
stress-induced tension
headaches.*

PROBLEM SOLVING

Sometimes we all feel that too many problems are crowding in on us at once. They may be related problems, one triggering another, or they may be unrelated and just happen to coincide at the same time. The result is that your head spins and your mind cannot concentrate, and you can't seem to find any answers, however hard you try.

SORTING AND PRIORITIZING

Perhaps you are "trying" too hard, rushing about so much that you are not giving yourself enough time to think logically. Take a few calming breaths, sit down comfortably with a pen and sheet of paper, a warm drink or fruit juice, and begin some logical problem-solving.

You need to keep in mind that you always have choices; you can change the situation; change yourself, or your way of viewing the situation; change neither, but calmly accept the way things are.

With this in mind, make a list of all the immediate problems which are stressing you—plus any other, minor problems which those are triggering. In the margin, put a number 1 by the side of the most urgent or stressful problem. That's the one to start with! On the other side of the sheet, write down how you would like to deal with this problem. Is this action possible? If you can say "yes," act on it! Action reduces stress! Or it may be more sensible to continue to examine your other problems; you may be able to deal with several at the same time.

If you have honestly to say "no," what would be your *next* preferred way to deal with the problem? Continue seeking solutions until you find one that you *can* implement; underline

◀ *It's easy to feel stressed, faced with a chaotic jumble of problems. Knowing where to begin is the first step in problem-solving.*

that one, and either act on it immediately or keep it ready for action while you look for ways of dealing with your other problems.

Decide which is the second most stressful or pressing problem on your list, and continue the same solution-finding procedures until you have solutions for most of your problems.

You will often find that what solves one problem also eases another. When you have finished this process to your satisfaction, you can begin to implement some of the solutions to your problems. Some cannot always be tackled immediately—the next day or the next week may be more appropriate for moving your plans on, but now at least you have outlined the problem and you have plans which you can implement. This type of problem-solving approach can be used either at home or in the workplace.

▼ *Breaking down your problems into a series of smaller tasks can make them seem less daunting. You can then deal with each problem in turn.*

SOMETIMES WHAT APPEARS TO BE ONE BIG PROBLEM...

is really a series of small problems ... stuck together.

If you can ...

untangle these small problems ...

you will find that some can be dealt with quite easily.

Tackle these first, and get them out of the way ...

then tackle the others, one by one.

But remember, you are only responsible for your own problems ...

not other people's ...

YOU CANNOT SOLVE THE PROBLEMS OF THE WHOLE WORLD.

BE ASSERTIVE

Being assertive allows you to express your thoughts, needs, feelings, and opinions, calmly and without aggression, without shouting and without whining. If you are passive, you may find that people walk all over you, and load more and more tasks onto you, until you reach breaking point.

This makes you feel stressed and in the long term does not really help others. On the other hand, by being aggressive you will promote avoidance or aggressive behaviors in others, which will also cause you stress. You need to tread the middle path, that of assertiveness. You are a person in your own right, entitled to as much consideration as anyone else, as long as you are willing to take the consequences of your own actions.

WHEN TO BE ASSERTIVE

Many people feel stressed because they are simply doing too much for others: in the work-place, "helping out colleagues" by doing extra work; in the home, doing things for everyone else in the family so that their lives will run smoothly. By doing this your own needs may remain unmet, and you will feel stressed.

Remember, you have the right to say "yes" and "no" for yourself,

NEGOTIATING

There are times, of course, when we all need to negotiate, for example, when something is "your job," but you do not want to do it now, or in that way. Alternatively you may want something done, which you could insist on aggressively, but it is far better to negotiate assertively, to promote a win-win outcome.

In negotiation you will be able to:

Empathize	Really try to put yourself in the other person's shoes. Acknowledge the other person's feelings: "I can see this is important to you …" "I can see that you are busy…"
Keep calm	Relax, and remember your breathing techniques.
Ask for clarification	Make sure you fully understand the other person's position. Understand their reasoning and their needs.
Be prepared	Take with you any facts and figures. Know what you are going to say.
Keep to the point	Beware of becoming sidetracked. Make sure the other person keeps to the point, too.
Offer a compromise	Look for the middle ground acceptable to both parties. It's there somewhere! Don't always expect everything your own way.

without giving reasons or making excuses. You have the right to be treated with respect as an equal, and you have a responsibility to respect the rights of others. You have the right to express your feelings and opinions in a calm and non-aggressive way. You have the right to say you don't understand, and to ask for more information. You have the right to choose not to be responsible for other people's problems. You do not need the approval of other people for your actions, provided you are willing and able to take the responsibility for the possible consequences yourself.

Be yourself, assertively.

◀ *Exude confidence, be strong in your self-esteem— above all be assertive, always remembering your rights as an individual.*

ASSERTIVE BEHAVIORS

When you are being assertive, you will have a calm and controlled voice; a relaxed but upright posture; and direct eye contact.

You will use the appropriate assertive words and phrases, such as "I want …," "I need …," "I think …," "I feel …"

You will want to involve the other person as well, saying things like: "Let us …" "How can we resolve this?" "What do you think?" "How do you see this?"

MANAGING ANGER

The emotional experience of anger is very stressful, whether it is your own anger, or being at the receiving end of someone else's anger. Angry situations need to be understood and dealt with sympathetically if the people concerned are all going to keep their self-respect and not come away from the situation suffering from stress.

Maybe you are expecting a confrontation shortly which is likely to culminate in an angry scene. Maybe you have just experienced one that you feel was unfair and you were not able to present your point of view. You may feel you would like to return to have

◀ *Even if you feel like snarling, stay calm and try to manage your anger.*

your say, but the prospect of encountering more anger is too stressful. On the other hand, smarting under an injustice is stressful, too.

MANAGING YOUR OWN ANGER

If you are feeling angry, make sure that you are in charge of and directing your anger, by being:

✴ assertive (you may need to read the section on assertiveness first, see pages 26–27)

✴ nonviolent

✴ goal-directed—know what you want to achieve and stick to the point

✴ ethical—don't use bully's tactics to get what you want.

✴ responsible—the outcomes are all down to you.

Stay calm, breathe regularly, and think before you speak. Also, remember to use assertiveness techniques. If you feel that you may "blow," say strongly and firmly, "I feel too angry to discuss this now; we will discuss this tomorrow at ten o'clock." This gives you both a cooling-off time, and a chance to marshal your facts and your thoughts.

MANAGING OTHER PEOPLE'S ANGER

If you are in a situation in which someone is angry with you, and demonstrating that anger, or if you have to return to an "angry" situation, there are a number of things you can do which will not only reduce your stress, but also reduce the stress (and thereby the anger) of the other person:

✴ Admit the feelings of the other person: "I can see that you are angry …"

✴ Admit the legitimacy of these feelings: "I can see that you feel very strongly about this …"

✳ But remember, you are not responsible for that person's feelings, s/he is.

✳ Admit your own feelings and responses: "I find that I am also getting angry and I'm afraid that I shall start saying things I may regret later." Do not say, "You are making me angry," or you are then trying to load your own feelings onto the other person.

✳ Postpone what seems to be an unproductive session, when the person is so angry you are making no progress. Say: "I know you are angry, but we can discuss this tomorrow." This gives you time to get your facts together, and the other person time to cool down.

✳ Angry people often come out with unfair criticism; you cannot reason with the unreasonable, so try a new approach. Turn the tables by agreeing with them: "I know I can be very selfish sometimes…" "I know I have made mistakes in the past…" "Perhaps it's true that I take you for granted…" They may find it difficult to argue against this; but if they become more aggressive, revert to "postponement."

▲ *Turn the tables on an angry person by making a gesture of appeasement.*

✳ Justifiable criticism and anger, or criticism which strikes home and wounds, is more difficult to deal with. Calmly agree with your critic, in a serious matter-of-fact tone, without adding any self put-downs or head-beatings, then find a way of making retribution which is agreeable to both of you. If you deny and bluster when you know the criticism is justified, the other person will become more angry.

BE READY

If you have to enter what you know will be an angry situation, or are going back to have your say, prepare yourself beforehand. On one side of a piece of paper, write down any criticisms which you might have had, or might expect to receive. On the other side, write your assertive, self-protective replies. Read and re-read these responses a number of times; you then have them ready if you need to use them, at any time:

✳ Prepare what you want to say.

✳ Rehearse the scene.

✳ Give yourself some positive self-talk.

✳ Relax your body (remember your breathing).

✳ Initiate a discussion when *you* are ready.

✳ Be ready for a defensive, angry reaction.

✳ Ask for clarification of their grievances; you may need to allow them time to offer explanations.

✳ Plan a reward for yourself when you have finished the task.

TIME PRIORITIES

It is very stressful to feel that you are pressed for time. You often hear people say there are not enough hours in the day. What would they do if they had more? Cram in a few more jobs? Occasionally, however, we all get frantically busy days, when everything happens at once. Maybe you are having just such a day today, and just need some help to get through it. Fine, we can do that.

MAKING A LIST

The first thing to do is to stop running around like a headless chicken and sit down calmly to make a list of what has to be done by the end of the day. Then read it through to see whether any items can be left to another day. If so, cross them off your list. If necessary, make a few phone calls to let people know that these will be dealt with tomorrow (it is always better to tell people this in advance, rather than having them phone you to ask what is happening).

So the remaining items on your list are essential for today. Now decide which of those tasks you could delegate to someone else. Even if you normally cover everything personally, today is different. Call in favors owed you; the neighbor whose children you picked up from school last week can be requested to get your children today. The friend who has just called to say his car has broken down outside of town will have to wait for the breakdown services to rescue him. The person who called your office to say she was "just passing but needed to see you for two minutes" could see your secretary instead.

PRIORITIZING YOUR TASKS

Now you are down to the jobs which really need your personal attention. Give those priority numbers, in the margin. Work out a realistic time that each job will take you. From this you can devise a timetable for yourself for the day—then stick to it! Don't let anyone else intrude, don't allow unexpected

TO SUMMARIZE

✷ Make a list of all you think you need to do.

✷ Cross off things which can be left for another time.

✷ Delegate those which can be done by others.

✷ Calculate time for each job left for you to do.

✷ Decide which order to do them in, bearing in mind the deadlines for each job.

✷ As you finish each job, reward yourself with a break—something to eat, something to drink, a few breaths of fresh air, a short two-minute relaxation exercise. (See pages 14–15.)

appointments, friends, or even business colleagues to distract you from it—it may seem like a welcome break at the time, but it will reduce your timetable which will only make you feel stressed again. Explain to callers (or, better still, have someone else explain to them) that you are tied up, but will be delighted to see them tomorrow, next week, next time they are in the area. Don't worry, they will understand—most people get days like this.

You can also save time by keeping things simple. For example, you may have planned to cook a very elaborate meal at the

◀ If you are acutely aware of time pressures and they are causing you to feel stressed, you may need to sort out your priorities.

end of the day for some friends whom you haven't seen for a long time; better than canceling your get-together, order something in, or do a simple meal. Your friends want to see you, not your kitchen!

GETTING STARTED

When you have prioritized and simplified jobs, you can begin your tasks. Sometimes the task of prioritizing shows you where you can dovetail jobs; work done on one job can actually be used toward another. A little planning goes a long way, but often we do not allow ourselves time for planning — which results in extra work!

What about the jobs which take longer than you allocated on your timetable? Was it that you had miscalculated the time necessary, or you didn't have all the information at hand, or

perhaps there was an equipment breakdown? It may be the prompt you need to say "I have spent long enough on this task." Nothing in life is perfect.

AT THE END OF THE DAY

Congratulate yourself on your achievements—but if all your days are this frantic, you need to take a fresh look at your life and make some fundamental changes. Take a course in time management, ask for extra staff, take on paid help in the home. There is no legislation to say that you must work yourself into a hole! You—and others around you—will benefit from your adoption of a less-frenetic lifestyle. You owe it to yourself and them.

11

POSITIVE THOUGHTS

Frequently we induce stress in ourselves by focusing on negative thoughts: "I am useless ..." "I can't do anything right ..." "My life is chaos ..." These negative thoughts may be the result of a chance remark from someone in our past; we store them and keep repeating them to ourselves until we believe them. Thinking positively about ourselves becomes more and more difficult.

OPPOSING YOUR NEGATIVE THOUGHTS

Maybe there is something specific, some negative thought or perception which is the cause of your stress today. Maybe you have been asked to do something which really you would like to do, but a negative perception of yourself is holding you back.

Identify your negative thought, and look at it objectively, then arrange the direct opposite

in your mind, and repeat this to yourself several times with more and more conviction. For example, you may have been asked to give a talk to a local group; your negative thought is: "I shall be useless at this." The positive thought is: "I shall be good at this." You can give yourself extra affirmation by adding, "They would not have asked me if they didn't think I could do it." If you need even more back-up, you can add, "I know the topic well" and "I shall enjoy this." But your main thought, which you need to keep repeating, is the one which directly opposes your immediate negative thought: "I shall be good at this." In your job and the activities that you do, try

◀ *Before negative thoughts intrude into your mind, examine them and reject them.*

saying to yourself, "I am enjoying this task." Initially you may lack conviction, but keep saying it and suddenly you will realize it is true. Instilling ideas into the subconscious is a very powerful mechanism, used by hypnotists, religious organizations, and many others. Take control for yourself and instill positive ideas about yourself; give yourself positive affirmations. Even if you don't believe them initially, you will gradually find that they will have an effect on you and you will start to live them. Wherever possible, keep your affirmations in the present tense, so that your subconscious believes they are true *now*. If you use the words "will" or "shall," your positive thoughts about yourself will stay in the future, out of reach.

Here are some positive affirmations. Try repeating them to yourself, or aloud if you would like to:

✳ Every day I am more and more confident.

✳ I can do my job as well as anyone else can.

✳ I am feeling strong.

✳ I am feeling calm, confident, or healthy (any positive word which you would like to apply to yourself).

✳ Every day my health is better and better.

✳ Every day my value as an individual increases.

✳ Every day my life is more and more fulfilling.

✳ I am feeling peaceful.

✳ I am feeling wonderfully invigorated.

Which one of these phrases would you like to feel is true of you? How do you need to feel today? Perhaps you can think of your own phrase. Keep repeating the phrase you select and feel your mood begin to lift. Promise yourself you will repeat it every day, at least ten times.

◀ Replace negative thoughts with positive ideas. Think about positive achievements and aspirations.

AFFIRMING OTHERS

Positive affirmations are funny things—they even work for you when you "give them away." If you say to a friend, "You are the kindest person I know" (provided you mean it, or they will detect a lie), not only will they feel good for receiving your affirmation, but you will feel good about giving it. We tend to complain more than we give praise, which can't be good for our inner feelings. Next time you receive good service, or buy what turns out to be a particularly good piece of merchandise, give affirmation to the seller or the person providing the service; they will probably be surprised, but certainly pleased, and you will also feel good about their feelings. Happiness spreads!

CHAPTER 2

WHAT IS STRESS?

This chapter looks at the causes of stress recognizing what is causing us stress is part-way to putting it right. Sometimes we

feel that our lives are in such a muddle that everything is stressful, but this is not really so; we need to separate out the real problems from the "just another thing to do" element, and find some semblance of order again. Recognizing when we are under stress, especially when our first symptoms appear, is important so that we can make a timely intervention. This chapter therefore also

offers a number of lifestyle-changing techniques, and suggests how to select the right stress-reducing technique for specific symptoms.

WHAT CAUSES STRESS?

The causes of stress vary quite widely from one person to another. We do not all find the same things stressful, just as we do not all find the same things pleasurable. Serious health problems in the family, or bereavement, are obviously stressful for everyone, but day-to-day problems with noise, traffic, or the children, for example, affect people differently.

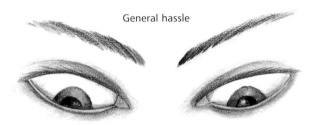
General hassle

Divorce

LIFE EVENTS

Major life events—both those which are perceived as "positive" as well as "negative"—may be stressful to a greater or lesser degree. Divorce or marriage, being pregnant or not being pregnant, moving house, children growing up and moving away—or not moving away—are among the many life changes that can lead to stress.

AT HOME

Families are often a source of stress, and this is the type of stress which has to be "managed" because we would not want to get rid of our family! Personal relationships, too, can be a source of great tension. Problems with loved ones, friends, or neighbors are stressful because we do not want a permanent rift to develop, and need to resolve the problem for both sides.

AT WORK

Work problems

Stress in the workplace may arise through having too much work to do, or work that is too difficult (these are both called "work overload"). "Work underload" brings its own stress. Work which is too easy is boring and therefore stressful. If there is not enough work to fill the day, that can also be stressful, and there may even be the threat of losing your job. Personality clashes in the workplace also cause strain, whether with the boss or a colleague who has to be encountered every day. Bullying in the workplace, as anywhere, is undoubtedly stressful and usually has repercussions on an individual's

Moving house

health. Bullying should not be tolerated under any circumstances; most organizations or trades unions have procedures for dealing with bullies, and they should be reported at the first opportunity, as should sexist or racist behavior, or verbal abuse.

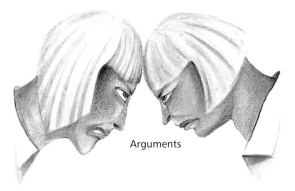
Arguments

DAY-TO-DAY HASSLES

Everyday events, if they irritate us and happen often, cause us to feel hassled. The neighbor's dog which keeps barking, driving to work in heavy traffic, someone else's badly behaved children, these may all seem minor on a good day, but when they are persistent or combine with other adverse events, they may become the last straw!

Stressors are cumulative—they add up. When we go to work, we take our "home" stressors with us; if we then have problems at work which can't be solved, the stress seems inescapable. This is why we need to manage our stress, possibly change or adapt our lifestyle a little, and learn to "work around" the problems we cannot solve.

Noise pollution

WHAT IS HAPPENING TO ME?

When we are stressed we all wonder this, not only because of the problems which are causing us the stress, but also because we do not understand the changes that are going on within ourselves. These may be physical, psychological, behavioral—or, most probably—a combination of all three.

A number of symptoms can arise, which are easily recognizable, but you may not have attributed them to stress; some may be the same as symptoms of particular illnesses, so if you are unsure, you may need to see your doctor. Whatever is causing you stress, the signs and symptoms are likely to be similar. As individuals we all have our own set of responses; some people's first sign is a headache, others find themselves becoming very irritable, and so on. Once you learn to recognize your stress symptoms and to manage your stress more effectively, you can reduce many of the symptoms without resorting to medication.

The checklist on pages 38–39 will help you to identify signs of stress and to choose those techniques best suited to relieve particular symptoms. This is followed by some explanations of what is going on within you, both mentally and physically, making you feel like this. Having worked your way through these, you can then turn to the rest of the book to find stressbusting solutions and suggestions for possible lifestyle changes that will help you to avoid problems in the future. You will find the most benefit from techniques which suit you as an individual! Try them and see.

SIGNS AND SYMPTOMS OF STRESS

The following are all stress symptoms: do you have any of them? Rate your own symptoms on a ten-point scale, putting 0 for the ones you never experience, up to 10 for the ones you experience a great deal of the time. In a few weeks, when you have used some of the stressbusting techniques in this book, re-rate your symptoms and see if they have subsided.

SYMPTOM	YOUR RATING		STRESSBUSTERS TO TRY
	NOW	1 MONTH	
Anxiety			Relaxation, rational thinking, herbalism, aromatherapy
Depression			Exercise, T'ai Chi, visualization
Negative thinking			Visualization, positive thinking, rational thinking
Increased alcohol consumption			Hypnotherapy, counseling
Insomnia			Relaxation, aromatherapy, herbalism, T'ai Chi
Sleeping too much			Exercise, Yoga, meditation
Overeating (especially sweet foods)			Healthy eating, exercise, visualization
Lack of appetite			Healthy eating, relaxation, counseling
Nausea			Relaxation, meditation, healthy eating, Yoga
Aching joints			Osteopathy, relaxation
Backache			Osteopathy, relaxation, Yoga, T'ai Chi
Smoking			Hypnotherapy, exercise, relaxation, meditation
Palpitations			Relaxation, Yoga

▶ *Stress affects different people in a variety of ways: by recognizing your own pattern of symptoms, you can learn to deal with stress promptly and effectively.*

Depression

Oversleeping

Turning to alcohol

SYMPTOM	YOUR RATING		STRESSBUSTERS TO TRY
	NOW	1 MONTH	
Breathlessness			Relaxation, T'ai Chi
Headaches			Relaxation, Yoga, massage
Anger			Meditation, relaxation, T'ai Chi, rational thinking
Tension			Meditation, massage
Irritability			Relaxation, massage, Yoga, aromatherapy
"Itchy" skin (generalized over body)			Relaxation, Yoga, exercise, T'ai Chi
Skin problems			Relaxation, Yoga, exercise, T'ai Chi
Allergies			Relaxation, exercise
Indigestion			Healthy eating, relaxation, herbalism, reflexology
Diarrhea			Healthy eating, relaxation, herbalism
Constipation			Healthy eating, exercise, relaxation, meditation
Insecurity			Assertiveness, Yoga, counseling, rational thinking
Loss of libido			Relaxation, counseling, reflexology, herbalism
Constant tiredness, fatigue			Relaxation, exercise, osteopathy, aromatherapy
Hyperactivity			Aromatherapy, herbalism, relaxation, exercise
"Fuzzy" head			Exercise, relaxation, herbalism, reflexology
Always in a hurry			Time management, T'ai Chi, relaxation
Too much to do			Time management
Continually harassed			Relaxation, Yoga, time management

Anger

Smoking

Headaches

PSYCHOLOGICAL RESPONSES TO STRESS

Our psychological responses include thoughts, memories, emotional responses (sudden surges of feeling), and these all influence the ways we, as individuals, cope with stress.

THOUGHT PROCESSES

We may assume that we are in charge of what we think, but this is not always true. How often has something popped into your head and you have said to yourself, "What a ridiculous thing to think?" This happens to everyone—we all have unconscious thought processes which suddenly make themselves conscious, often as strange or irrelevant thoughts. When we are under stress, we are likely to take these odd thought processes seriously, instead of examining them in a rational and calm way. The technique described under *Replacing Irrational Thoughts* on page 84 explains how to do this.

MEMORIES

We begin learning from an early age, and those early learning processes form memories. Some may be forgotten, some may be stored subconsciously. Unpleasant occurrences tend to make a great impression on us, especially in childhood. Because of the impact they made at the time, memories of those occurrences are often pushed to the back of our minds. When another unpleasant event occurs, such as something stressful, all the memories and associated emotions come crowding back to us.

This is why, when you are feeling depressed, you can seem to think only of other depressing events which happened in the past, maybe years ago. You know there is nothing you can do about

▲ *Emotions associated with past unpleasant experiences are ready to surface again when triggered by another traumatic experience.*

the past events, but they won't seem to leave you alone. The way to deal with this situation is to go for a walk, and use some positive thinking to put the past events from you, and then use some problem-solving techniques (see pages 24–25) to deal with the current events.

EMOTIONAL RESPONSES

We like to think that as we grow up we have more control over our emotions—we no longer blush when embarrassed, or kick and scream when things go wrong. In fact, what we are probably doing is controlling our responses, but the emotions are still occurring inside us; there is still that little boy or little girl in there, trying to get out! We still get just as upset over sad events, just as elated when everything goes right, only we just don't show it so readily. This fits in better with our adult environment.

What is bad for us is to deny that these emotions actually exist. We need to acknowledge that we have feelings—as do other people. I am not advocating that you cry in public if this would embarrass you, but you should always feel free to cry in private. Denial of our own emotions leads us to feel even more stress. We need to be able to say, "I am happy, I am sad, I am angry," and not feel guilty about it. If things have all gone horribly wrong for you, go and shut yourself in a room and have a good scream (as Japanese businessmen do!). You will feel much better when you have released the emotions, and will then be able to begin your rational, problem-solving approach to whatever is causing you stress.

COPING WITH STRESS

As individuals we all have different methods of coping with stress. A great deal of the investigative work into coping methods has been done in conjunction with bereavement. At one time it was thought that people coped best with bereavement by being immensely practical and getting on with their lives in a "normal" way. More recent research suggests that these are the people who are not coping well—they are the ones who show stress and become ill later. We all really need grieving time, to cry, to show emotions, to think about the person we have lost, and then, when we are ready, we can pick up the practicalities of life. Of course, it is not useful to allow the grieving process to go on too long; help may be needed from counselors or friends in order to strike a balance.

Some ways of coping with stress are emotion-focused, others are problem-focused. It is thought to be healthy to use a little of both.

► *We all have individual ways of coping with stress. Emotional release is often necessary before we can move onto problem-solving methods of coping with our stress.*

COMMON COPING STRATEGIES

Emotion-focused

✳ Seeking support and sympathy from friends

✳ Having a good cry, or scream

✳ Having a good laugh

✳ Pretending it hasn't happened

✳ Praying for guidance

These may only be of use temporarily, but may be absolutely essential to get over an initial shock. You may need to move on to one of these:

▼ *One calming process is to visualize a restful place: when you feel calm you can begin to cope with solving stressful problems. (See pages 88–89.)*

Problem-focused

✳ Seeking information and practical help

✳ Regarding this as a learning experience, and being positive about it

✳ Planning how to remove or get around the problem

✳ Realizing that there is nothing you can do about the situation, and planning how you can live with it

Strategies that are not much help, either emotionally or for problem-solving, include heavy drinking or drugs—even prescription ones.

BEHAVIORAL RESPONSES TO STRESS

Some of the ways in which we behave, some of the actions we take, are stress-producing in themselves. These often become habits; for example, we may not need to rush around, but we have got into the habit of always hurrying. This serves to produce and maintain the body's stress responses.

TYPE-A BEHAVIOR

In the 1970s, psychologists identified a "type" of person who seemed always to be in a hurry, was hostile and aggressive, extremely competitive, both at work and in leisure activities, and seemed unable to "switch off" at all. These "Type-A" people, as they were called, were found to be more than twice as likely as anyone else to suffer from heart attacks. Although later information suggests that there is also a strong genetic link to heart attacks, these Type-A behaviors are best avoided.

Are you a Type-A? Try the quiz below and see how you score.

TESTING YOUR TYPE

Rate yourself on a ten-point scale on the following, scoring 0 for "not at all," and 10 for "all the time."

1 *Are you always rushed, in a hurry, under pressure?* _____

2 *Do you do more than one thing at a time?* _____

3 *Are you ambitious and competitive?* _____

4 *Do you find it impossible to wait patiently?* _____

5 *Do you finish other people's sentences for them?* _____

6 *Do you drive yourself (and other people) hard?* _____

SCORING

Now add up your score; if you scored more than 30 you are on the Type-A side. If you find that you are high on the Type-A scale, it might be worth examining your lifestyle, slowing down a bit, and not taking on so much.

▶ *Trying to do everything at once is an effective way of producing stress! By learning to prioritize tasks and delegate some jobs to other people, we can send calmer messages to our bodies.*

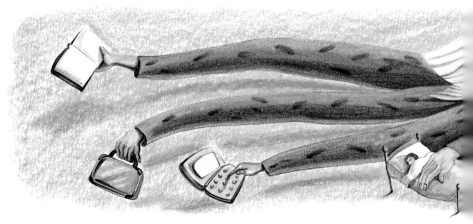

POOR TIME MANAGEMENT

Are you always in a hurry, yet don't seem to get much done? Are you constantly in a muddle? These things are stress-producing and could be solved by better time management and a little organization.

If you are constantly sending messages to your body that it has to speed up, because you are behind in what you are doing (or think you are), all the body's "activity" system is alerted. You are using up your body's precious resources, and will probably become very tired, which means in the end that you won't get everything done anyway! A little planning, list-writing, and delegation may solve a number of problems for you.

Long-term results of poor management include irritability, digestive upsets, and other physical symptoms. On the home front and in social situations, poor time management can cause disagreement and conflict; no one wants to socialize with a person who is constantly late, or frequently has to rearrange dates because they are always behind schedule. All of these results cause further stress to the already-stressed individual, so that stress becomes a vicious circle.

IS POOR TIME MANAGEMENT CAUSING YOU STRESS?

To answer each question, put a tick in the most appropriate box.

	NEVER	SOMETIMES	OFTEN	ALWAYS
1 Do you move back and forth from task to task?	☐	☐	☐	☐
2 Are you constantly retracing your steps?	☐	☐	☐	☐
3 Do you prefer to do jobs yourself, rather than passing them to others?	☐	☐	☐	☐
4 Do you spend too much time just chatting to colleagues?	☐	☐	☐	☐
5 Does the telephone constantly interrupt you?	☐	☐	☐	☐
6 Do you have to arrive at work early or stay late to complete everything?	☐	☐	☐	☐
7 Do you spend time searching for things you need?	☐	☐	☐	☐

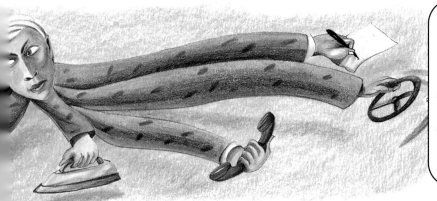

SCORING

If you have more of your responses in the Often and Always columns, some of your stress is almost certainly due to time pressure. Try looking at *Time Priorities* on pages 30–31, or *Managing Your Time Effectively* on pages 96–97.

LACK OF ASSERTIVENESS

Do you frequently find yourself doing things you don't want to do, often for other people? Do you feel you are being "dumped on," either at work, at home, or in your social sphere? If you do, it may be that you are not assertive enough.

Being assertive means being able to stand up for yourself, being able to say what you want or need or are willing to do, without shouting or aggression. You are a person in your own right, not there just to look after others. You need time and space just to "be." If you are usually acquiescent, people will ask you to do things for them—they won't ask the people who say no.

You need to learn to say "no." You don't have to give reasons for not doing something which is not your job; just calmly be firm and polite, but keep repeating "no." You have the same rights as everyone else, and others must learn to respect them. If you are continually putting yourself out for others, you will not have time for yourself, and your self-esteem will suffer; this is stressful in itself. If you need to change to more assertive behavior, read *Be Assertive* on page 26.

SMOKING

People who smoke often say that they do this because they are stressed. However, smoking causes poor health, from coughs and bronchitis to lung cancer. Smokers realize this, and—although they often do not admit it, even to themselves—this knowledge causes them more stress. So the very behavior which they adopted to reduce stress is, in fact, adding to it.

Giving up smoking is not easy; people become chemically addicted as well as psychologically addicted. The really strong, or those with a highly

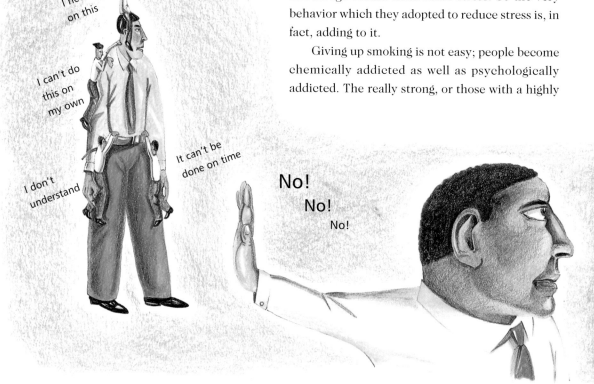

I need help on this

I can't do this on my own

I don't understand

It can't be done on time

No!
No!
No!

motivating reason, may manage to give up alone; others may need help, using chemical patches, hypnotherapy, or other forms of assistance. But it can be done!

ALCOHOL DEPENDENCE

Many people take a drink and can then leave it alone. There are some researchers who suggest that a modicum of alcohol is good for the health, although subsequent research suggested it was not the alcohol content in wine but chemicals in the grapes that were actually beneficial. However, up to 14 units of alcohol a week for a woman, and 21 for a man, is not thought to be detrimental to health. But people who reach for a drink every time there is any sort of problem maybe need to ask themselves why, or whether there is a better solution.

Alcohol may make things look better, but only for a very short time. It is, in fact, a central nervous system depressant: it acts to damp down mood, rather than uplift, which is really the last thing a stressed individual needs. Alcohol dependence is likely to be both a chemical and a psychological problem, which needs help. It is stressful not only for the individual concerned, but for his or her family, friends, and workmates. For those who recognize that they have a problem, Alcoholics Anonymous or trained counselors can provide help and experienced guidance.

When there is a crisis, then, rather than reach for the bottle, reach for one of the instant solutions in Chapter 1.

▼ *By learning to say "no" to unreasonable demands, we can free ourselves from many stressful problems. The way to do this is to use a positive, assertive approach. Smoking or alcohol dependence only masks problems, not solves them.*

PHYSICAL RESPONSES TO STRESS

Under stress, the body follows a specific set of responses. Incoming stress is registered by the brain, whether it is picked up by the eyes, the ears, or any of the other senses. The brain then sets off our automatic response system for dealing with stressors. This is still the same set of responses which were applied by early man—known as the "flight or fight" response—but we cannot always fight or run away from our particular stressor, so our responses may keep on revolving for some time, until we can reach some sort of solution.

MIND AND BODY

Because there is such a strong relationship between the mind and the body, events which affect the mind also affect the body, and vice versa. Stress certainly demonstrates this mind/body relationship, where any stressor, whether mental or physical, is reflected by responses from within the body.

There are two distinct yet coordinated systems which the brain activates under stress: one is the Autonomic Nervous System (ANS); the other is the hormonal or endocrine system. The ANS is activated more quickly, while the endocrine system is slower to start but runs on longer. If stress continues over a period of time, the immune system also becomes impaired, which can have disastrous effects on the individual.

THE NERVOUS SYSTEM UNDER STRESS

The ANS is a part of the body's nervous system which governs the soft tissues such as the digestive system, or organs such as the heart and the liver. When activated, it moves into "action mode," which speeds up or slows down the functioning of parts of the body, in order to prepare to fight, or run away.

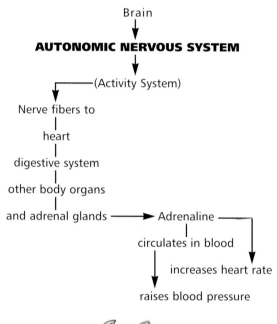

HOW THE NERVOUS SYSTEM IS INVOLVED IN STRESS REACTIONS

Brain
↓
AUTONOMIC NERVOUS SYSTEM
↓
(Activity System)

Nerve fibers to
heart
digestive system
other body organs
and adrenal glands ——→ Adrenaline ——
circulates in blood
increases heart rate
raises blood pressure

◀ There is a finely tuned balance between the mind and the body; too much stress is likely to produce "overload" and make the system collapse.

When danger is past, it enters "resting mode," enabling the body to return to a comfortable, resting state. These two modes cannot be activated together.

Ideally, as humans, we should have periods of activity and periods of resting in order to replenish the body. If we are under stress, the action mode is constantly activated and the systems it sends messages to are constantly on the alert. Any system which is constantly over-used runs the risk of breaking down. A number of the major organs are activated by the ANS, and these need to be protected as they are indispensable.

HOW THE ANS AFFECTS THE BODY

PART OF BODY	ACTION MODE (STRESS REACTION)
Heart	Increased rate
Blood vessels	Dilated, to increase blood flow to muscles
Pupils	Dilated, to aid vision
Gut	Movement and digestive processes slowed
Saliva glands	Decreased production
Bronchi (lungs)	Dilated, to aid breathing
Adrenal glands	Stimulated, to release adrenaline
Liver	Stores of glucose released, to increase energy levels
Skin	Increased sweating
Bladder, bowel	Relaxed, with possible temporary loss of control

Imagine this situation: You are walking down the street when you see a lion. You have the choice of running away or staying to fight. Your brain will make the conscious decision for you, but your ANS has already become mobilized, without needing conscious instruction.

Whichever alternative is chosen, activity is the order of the day, therefore the ANS speeds up the heart rate (remember, nerve impulses take only split seconds to travel), dilates the walls of the blood vessels to speed blood to the limbs, dilates the pupils so that you can see your adversary more clearly, releases glucose into the bloodstream for energy, and brings other changes into play which are advantageous for an active state.

The ANS also activates the adrenal glands, to release adrenaline into the bloodstream; it circulates to the heart, making the heart beat faster—very useful if you are about to run away or fight with a lion, but in a stressful eight-hour day at work, only makes you feel bad.

HORMONES UNDER STRESS

In addition to the activity of the ANS, the endocrine system brings a specific set of hormonal responses into play when stress occurs. The brain, on sensing stress, informs the pituitary gland, which sends hormonal messages to other glands in the body. Of particular importance is the hormone ACTH which it sends to the adrenal glands, causing them to release cortisol and sex hormones. The sex hormones, particularly testosterone, promote aggression, again very useful if you are fighting mad, but not in a situation where you need to control your anger. Cortisol is a hormone essential to life; it is one of the steroids and helps maintain the body's high response levels. Too little and the body does not function effectively; too much and it interferes

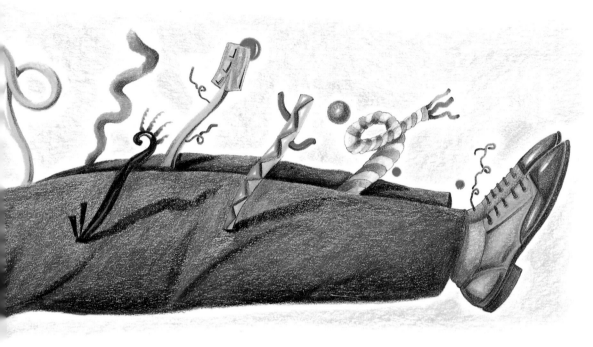

▲ *Discovering how the body responds to stress can help us recognize symptoms and their causes; reducing stress will reduce these physical reactions.*

HOW THE HORMONAL SYSTEM IS INVOLVED IN STRESS REACTIONS

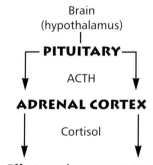

Brain
(hypothalamus)
|
┌── **PITUITARY** ──┐
↓   ↓
ACTH
↓   ↓
ADRENAL CORTEX
↓   ↓
Cortisol
↓   ↓

Effects on immune system
Reduction in circulating lymphocytes, thereby reducing the efficiency of the immune system.

with the immune system, which is essential for keeping us physically healthy.

When the body is under stress, too much cortisol is released, and in the long term this suppresses some of the cell production in the immune system. Consequently the immune system does not function properly, and you become susceptible to any germs which are circulating; this is why we so often pick up colds and 'flu when we are "down." The immune system also protects us against the "big" diseases, such as cancer.

THE EFFECTS OF CONTINUING STRESS

The reactions of the body under stress are triggered by either mental events which are unpleasant, or by other physical events in the body, such as serious illness or operations. When these stressors disappear, the body's stress responses will return to normal. If they do not disappear, the stress responses will continue, until all the body's resources are used up, and the individual will collapse.

CHAPTER 3

MANAGING STRESSFUL SITUATIONS

Sometimes situations arise which are stressful in themselves; these need to be managed promptly and effectively, in order  to prevent them from getting worse. Some situations may be expected—we may know when there is a confrontation looming at work, or at home. We can think this through and put our defenses in place, using some of the strategies outlined in this book. Other stressful situations may arise unexpectedly, whether at home,  at work, or socially. These are more difficult to manage, as we have not had time to prepare ourselves mentally.

CRISIS AT HOME
FINANCIAL

One of the fundamental underlying causes of family stress is money problems. Shortage of money, or one partner feeling that they are contributing more than the other, or that the other partner has spent more than their fair share of a joint income, or lack of power over saying how family money should be spent—all of these are causes of disagreement which can lead to ongoing stress.

EMOTIONAL INVOLVEMENT

It is important to recognize that emotions are involved in what seems like a very practical topic: money. For a partner who is no longer in paid employment, whether through being laid off or choice (perhaps in order to undertake childcare), there is a feeling of loss of status, especially if that person was previously a high earner. In adults, self-esteem and personal identity are often closely bound to the job an individual does; loss of that job means loss of part of the "self," with consequent loss of self-esteem as well as a new feeling—that of financial dependence on others. It is important that these partners are still involved in financial decisions, which were always part of their role.

▲ *Spending money without any thought or planning can be a recipe for disaster, invoking subsequent stress. Financial planning and making sure there is enough money for spending plans may seem boring but results in stress-free finances.*

DEALING WITH A FINANCIAL CRISIS

1 The first thing to do is make a realistic assessment of what you need to spend each month: rent, food, taxes, car expenses, gas, electricity, etc. (Don't forget to include items which only need paying once a year, such as insurance.)

2 Next make a realistic assessment of income per month. From this, make a fair assessment of what each person can be expected to contribute each month. If one person earns far more than the other, "fair" may not mean a 50/50 split. Perhaps an agreed percentage of income would be fairer.

3 Now arrange for those sums of money to be debited automatically from each account and placed into a joint, family "Budget" account, for the payment of the items agreed in step 1, above. Decide now whether one person will be responsible for actually drawing from that account to pay the bills, and if so, who? Or decide who will be responsible for paying separate items. Whatever you decide, stick to it!

NOT ENOUGH MONEY?

Maybe you have completed the first two steps and found that your income does not fully cover your expenditure. Drastic action is called for if domestic peace is to prevail!

1 Re-examine step 1: is all your expenditure absolutely necessary? Frequently there are items which seem essential when times are good but, when your circumstances change, these can be seen as non-essentials. For example, can the family do with one car less? If so, rational discussion, without anger, is needed to decide which one is dispensable. Or is the golf-club membership really necessary?

2 Whatever items have been identified as reducible or even dispensable, re-examine them, to see which family member will be most affected by each. The same family member should not be affected every time; no one should be expected to make all the sacrifices, which will lead to resentment and stress.

SEVEN-POINT PLAN

✳ Have a "family meeting" to discuss financial problems. Agree at the outset that people will not shout or accuse others; discussion has to be calm and rational.

✳ Involve all the adult members of the family, including adolescent children, even if they do not contribute to income. They need to understand problems of income/expenditure, and can often make useful suggestions—and sacrifices.

✳ Make sure all decisions are kept to; check up on each other—kindly, not accusingly.

✳ Review the financial situation every three or six months; you may need to make slight adjustments.

✳ If, after a joint family effort, you cannot find a way to straighten your family finances, seek the help of an expert. Make an appointment with a financial adviser, debt counselor, or ask your bank to suggest someone to advise on budgeting.

✳ If you have a cashflow problem, ask your bank about a short-term loan or overdraft facility. They are much happier to be asked than for you to overdraw without asking. As a rule, loans are cheaper than overdrafts.

✳ Don't let disagreements over money drive your family apart; discuss and keep discussing. Don't quarrel. If meetings get too heated, adjourn them to another day, and you can all do some thinking in the meantime.

MOVING HOUSE

Rated as one of the most stressful life events, there are many areas of stress associated with moving house. There are the emotional stresses associated with leaving a familiar place and entering a new one; there are the physical stresses of packing, sorting, and clearing rubbish. There are also cognitive stresses associated with trying to coordinate everything, remembering to contact utilities, and checking whether tasks have been carried out by other people.

EMOTIONAL STRESS

Even if you are pleased to be moving to a new home, there are always emotional ties to the old one, and sadness at leaving friends and neighbors as well. Do not underestimate the stress felt by children, who are leaving a familiar neighborhood, friends, and school. Their uncertainty, if not handled in a caring manner, may upset them for some months afterward. Make sure you find time to talk things through with them.

ORGANIZING TIMETABLES

It is very difficult to coordinate times for moving out of one house into another. If you are renting, the dates of leases have to coincide; if this becomes impossible, arrange to store furniture and stay in a hotel for a few days. This may be more expensive than staying with friends or relatives, but if you have a large family to move, it may be less stressful in the long term.

If you are selling one house and purchasing another, your lawyer will endeavor to tie in the dates together. That involves moving furniture out of one house, transporting it, and moving it into another house all in the same day; again, a break in a hotel may make this less frenetic.

Careful packing for several weeks before the move avoids a last-minute rush. There are sure to be items in your house which you could do without for several weeks; out-of-season clothes, for example, or the "best" china, family heirlooms, photographs, spare curtains, and linen. All these can be packed long before the week in which you are moving.

COLOR CODING

One thing I have done on several occasions, which seems to work well, is to buy different-color stickers for each room, for example, red for the study, yellow for the kitchen, blue for my bedroom, etc. As I pack a box, I stick that room's color on the box. When we arrive at the new house, I rush in before the movers arrive and place colored stickers on the doors of the rooms in which I want those boxes. This saves me from constantly having to direct boxes to specific areas; the moving men approve, too.

TIMETABLING FOR THE MOVE

✳ Coordinate dates with landlords, if renting, or through your lawyer, if purchasing.

✳ Order furniture removal vans as soon as you have some firm dates (some companies will accept provisional dates, to be confirmed later).

✳ Tell your bank you are moving, in case you have a last-minute cashflow problem.

✳ Take children to see the new neighborhood and new schools.

✳ Arrange for someone to care for family pets on the moving day, so you can pick them up later.

✳ Start packing several weeks before the event, so that *you* do not get overtired and stressed. Make sure you do not become obsessed with the move.

Two weeks to go make a timetable and list of jobs to be completed before moving, such as arranging to finalize old electricity/phone/gas supplies, and initiate new ones at the new house.

Final week finish packing; confirm arrangements for animals and children.

Moving day be prepared to leave it to your moving company; they are the experts, they do it every day. Organize the children and family pets. Only expect to put small items in the car with you, such as house plants (but keep everything you need for making a hot drink at the other end handy!).

And finally when you are in your new house, surrounded by boxes, do *not* attempt to cook a meal that night. Order in, or, better still, go out for a meal to a nice restaurant, perhaps have a bottle of wine, and drink a toast to your new home!

▼ *Moving house can be stressful, yet with a little planning everything can run smoothly. Incorporate all the family into the planning stage, so everyone feels involved from the beginning.*

STRESSBUSTING IN THE WORKPLACE

Stress at work can come from a number of sources: the job itself, the culture of the organization, other people (both colleagues and managers), and the physical work environment.

THE PHYSICAL ENVIRONMENT

Some years ago, open-plan offices were the new idea; it equalized the status of all the workers in the office. What sounded like a good idea was, in fact, counter-productive. The noise levels in large, open-plan offices are distracting and detrimental to productivity; and people like to work with a degree of privacy, and not for any underhand reasons. Big offices have been now partitioned into smaller units, where people feel more comfortable.

The permissible level of noise in the workplace is monitored by legislation, as are minimum and maximum temperatures. Employers must also supply adequate workspace with ergonomically sound furniture (in other words, the furniture must fit the worker). Machinery and equipment must comply with current safety standards. These rulings are designed to make the worker more comfortable, thereby ensuring that he or she suffers no physical stress. If you feel that these regulations are not enforced in your workplace, you should consult your trades union or workers council, who can take the matter to management on your behalf. Physical stress can lead to psychological stress, and both can lead to poor health.

WORK OVERLOAD OR UNDERLOAD?

Too much work, or work that is too difficult, is very stressful. Since "downsizing" became the method used by companies to save money, many employees have been asked to take on extra duties, over and above their own job. Sometimes the extra work is unfamiliar, or outside their area of expertise, but they dare not complain, in case they are next in line for "downsizing." As a result, they take work home, or work longer hours, and worry more—all very stressful. If the situation is allowed to continue, their physical and mental health suffers. They may begin to suffer from "job burnout," symptoms of which include pessimism, dissatisfaction, a feeling of no longer caring about the job, and taking days off through feeling "under par."

Wise employers have realized that downsizing that puts pressure on remaining staff is a false economy, because days are lost through stress. In addition, employees who suffer from stress through work can sue their employer; the employer has a legal obligation to care for employees' mental as well as physical health.

Work underload arises when the job is either too easy or there is not enough work to fill a day, both of which induce boredom that produces a different type of stress, but real, nonetheless. There is also the feeling that insufficient work may result in being laid off; again this is highly stressful.

◄ *Good work practices applied at each level of a company's hierarchy will go towards an efficient, relatively stress-free work force. If middle management staff are overloaded with work and stressed this will move down through lower levels in the hierarchy, and vice versa.*

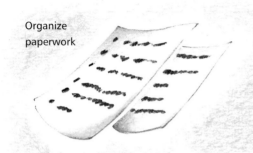

Organize
paperwork

Delegate tasks

Contact a work
counselor

HOW WELL ARE YOU COPING AT WORK?

We all need a challenge at work, but too much becomes stressful. Find out how well
you are coping at work: answer "yes" or "no" to the following questions.

1 *I feel enthusiasm for my job.* _____

2 *I feel my efforts at work are appreciated.* _____

3 *I feel tired at work, even after a night's sleep.* _____

4 *I am forgetful.* _____

5 *Recent changes at work have been for the better.* _____

6 *I can communicate easily with colleagues and supervisors.* _____

7 *I feel a sense of dissatisfaction most of the time.* _____

8 *I feel emotionally, physically, or spiritually depleted.* _____

9 *My health is not as good as it was six months ago.* _____

10 *I am not as efficient as I would like to be.* _____

SCORING

If you have answered "no" to
questions 1, 2, 5, 6, score 1 point
each. If you have answered "yes" to
questions 3, 4, 7, 8, 9, 10, score 1
point each. Now add your total.

8 TO 10 POINTS

You are burning out, and need to make
a comprehensive plan—see the
Stressbuster Plan opposite.

4 TO 7 POINTS

You are probably suffering from some
job-related stress and need to take
preventive action.

1 TO 3 POINTS

You seem to be coping adequately with
your job.

▲ ▶ *Find the best
solution to your
workplace problem,
for you as an
individual. What
suits your colleague
may not suit you, as
we are all different.*

STRESSBUSTER PLAN

✷ Make a list of what you find stressful at work.

✷ Decide which of the items on your list you can change for yourself. Can you improve your time management skills, or delegate work more effectively?

✷ If you feel that you are being bullied at work, act immediately. Go to your union or phone your local helpline; no one has to put up with bullying or harassment in the workplace.

✷ If certain colleagues are causing you stress, work out a plan for having minimal contact with them. Spend more time with those you find relaxing, encouraging, and appreciative.

✷ Decide which items on your "stress list" could be changed by your organization; see your manager with a plan of action you would propose.

✷ If he or she ignores you, enlist the help of colleagues, or try a higher level of management, your human resources department, or your union.

✷ You may not manage to get everything changed, but give the new changes a while and see how you feel. You may decide to see a counselor—many organizations employ them. You may be able to participate in stress management programs at work. If all else fails, you may decide to look for a new job elsewhere.

Keeping the peace at work

Social contact with colleagues you like is relaxing

KNOWING WHEN TO QUIT

If you feel you have made as many adaptations as you can at work and are still feeling stressed, ask yourself if the job is worth all the emotional upheaval it costs you. Do you also feel that your physical health is suffering? Do you go home so tired and dispirited that you are irritable and cannot enjoy life? If so, maybe now is the time to find a new job. Organizations which have a great deal of internal dissatisfaction and stress are usually those in trouble. If they do not choose to put this right, they may fold, so better to get out sooner than later.

SOCIAL SITUATIONS
ENTERTAINING

Whether you actively want to entertain, or whether you reluctantly do so because you feel obligated, both can be stressful. There is always the worry that guests may not "get along" together, that the food may be a disaster, or that a small thing could go wrong. The secret is good organization. Careful planning ensures that everything runs smoothly.

GETTING ORGANIZED

Send out invitations, or make phone calls for an informal occasion, in plenty of time. Most people like to organize their social calendar well in advance; some also need to arrange for babysitting. Plan menus well in advance and try out anything new on the family first. This gives you the confidence to know that you can do it—and how long it takes!

A great deal of preparation can be done the day before; some can be done the week before and frozen until required. Don't be too ambitious; go for a cold first course so you can spend some time with your guests when they first arrive. They are coming to see you, not test your skills as a cook! If you are making a meal with several courses, plan a careful "cooking timetable" for the day, to make sure that all the food is ready at the same time.

Two days before the event, clean the rooms you will be using. Make sure that glasses, dishes, and utensils are sparkling clean. Also remember to clean your front entrance and make it welcoming.

One day before the event, go through your menu and write down everything you will need for each dish. Check your cupboards—never assume you have all the ingredients you need. Do the shopping for those items you need. Prepare as many dishes in advance as you can. Arrange fresh flowers.

On the day itself, take frozen items from the freezer for defrosting; prepare any vegetables and fruit; lay the table. Open red wines, and chill white wines. Consult your cooking timetable, and stick to it. To keep your work environment as clear as possible, wash used utensils as you go.

And finally, *enjoy yourself*! If anything does go wrong, it is not the end of the world; tell your guests about it and you can all have a laugh!

▼ *If you are unsure of your abilities as a host or hostess, choose something simple, such as drinks and snacks, for a first occasion. It is better to do something simple well than something complex badly!*

A QUESTION OF CONFIDENCE

If we are confident, we can do anything! Try the following questionnaire, to rate your own self-esteem. Tick "agree" or "disagree" for each statement.

AGREE   DISAGREE

1 *Most of my friends are more interesting than I am.*

2 *Most people I know seem to have a high regard for me.*

3 *I sometimes feel excluded from my circle of friends.*

4 *I am usually successful in making changes in my life.*

5 *I have achieved a number of things through skill and hard work.*

6 *I seem to lack the ability to control social situations.*

7 *I cannot seem to guide the course of a conversation, even with friends.*

SCORING

Score 1 point each if you have ticked "disagree" for statements 1, 3, 6, 7, and "agree" for statements 2, 4, 5.

5 TO 7 POINTS

You have no problems with self-esteem. You can probably handle social situations well.

4 TO 5 POINTS

Your self-esteem is O.K.; you may need some practice in social skills, but they should not be too stressful.

1 TO 3 POINTS

You need to give yourself some positive affirmations (see page 33). Remember, you are as good as anyone else. Also look at *Be Assertive* (see pages 26–27), which may be an underlying problem. Then tackle small situations first, gradually giving yourself greater challenges as your confidence increases.

BIG OCCASIONS

If it is a special occasion such as your birthday or wedding, you cannot help but be the center of everyone's attention. Remember, they all want it to be a success for you; no one would want to see you put down on your big day. You probably look your best, too, with new clothes and a rosy glow which goes with the excitement of a big occasion. Give yourself some positive affirmations before you start meeting people, then—relax and enjoy!

If you have to make a speech, prepare it. Very few people are born orators who can talk brilliantly without preparation. On the other hand, don't write a speech and then proceed to read it word-for-word; your audience wants to see your eyes, not the top of your head! Simply jot down a few main topics (or people) you want to mention, and say a little about each one. If you have rehearsed first, your speech will be more fluent, and strangely enough will seem more spontaneous. Rehearse it in front of a mirror, then you can see what you look like during delivery. Or if you can find a willing listener or two, rehearse it in front of them.

Think positive thoughts: if it is your wedding or birthday, you are not going to be alone on the edge of a crowd; no one will forget you are there!

MEETING NEW PEOPLE

The "big" occasions are often when you will meet a number of people you do not already know. It may help you to be less worried if you realize that they

are probably just as nervous about meeting you as you are about meeting them, and you are all trying desperately not to show it.

When you are being introduced to someone new, take a deep breath before you speak; it will give you enough voice to say "hello" confidently. If you are worried about forgetting a person's name, try repeating it to yourself, under your breath, and add a reminder, such as "Anna—has red hair," or "George—looks like Uncle Fred." If you do forget names, don't worry; but don't avoid the person because you have forgotten their name—they may be really interesting. You can always quietly ask for a reminder from the person who first introduced you. Or you can talk to them without using their name, in the hope that someone else will come along and say it.

If you can never think of suitable topics of conversation with new people, have a few prepared topics ready to produce. If you have read an interesting novel recently, or watched a good program on T.V., you may find that you have common ground here. Try not to be too domineering in your views, however—you are only making conversation, not writing a thesis!

If you find that you avoid new social situations, try to challenge yourself with an achievable goal. Challenge yourself to go into a new situation and stay there for ten minutes; after that you are free to leave, because you have achieved your goal. Next time, challenge yourself to stay longer!

▼ *If you find being the center of attention intimidating, remember that the people there are really on your side; no one is looking for your downfall. Take some slow breaths and smile.*

CHAPTER 4

STRESS MANAGEMENT

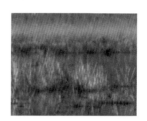

Ideally, stress should be removed at source. But we don't live in an ideal world, and not all problems can simply be wiped away. In any case we don't really want to remove all the challenges from our lives, just the "overload," which becomes stressful. So we need to find ways of managing our stressful situations and our own stress responses. The following pages suggest ways and techniques for doing this. Some need practice, some produce immediate benefits which increase as you continue to use them. These are systems to

incorporate into your lifestyle, to help create a stress-proof you!

T'AI CHI

T'ai Chi comes from China, where one of the fundamental beliefs is that there are "energy channels" which flow around the body. If these are not kept clear, the *chi*, or intrinsic energy of the body, cannot flow, and the individual will suffer as a consequence.

T'ai Chi consists of a series of movements which are calm, deliberate, and flow from one to another. Originally, T'ai Chi was a martial art; the movements originated from warriors' battle movements. However, these emphasize blending the skills of the mind with the skills of the body, using the mind to control the violence of the body, so mind and body are treated as one.

Although the technique is better taught through classes and interpersonal contact, you will find some excellent books on the subject. T'ai Chi requires focused attention, so stressful thoughts are squeezed out, and regular practice imparts a sense of calm to people in their daily lives.

One way of practicing is to make sure that all movements and tasks throughout the day are done with the same quiet, deliberate movement, and all given full attention. Paying this kind of attention to a physical activity calms the brain patterns, thereby leading to greater control over the emotions—which, in turn, means taking greater control of your life.

▶ *T'ai Chi is performed as a series of controlled, precise movements. The series of steps shown here is one of the linking movements in a complete routine which a qualified teacher would show you in a supervised class.*

1 *With knees bent, take your weight onto your left leg. Your forearms are crossed in front of your chest.*

2 *Raise your arms in front to slightly above shoulder level, palms facing outward. Lift your right knee, toes pointing down.*

3 *Now gently kick out with your right foot slowly, pointing toes. Now swivel your raised right leg and body towards the right, while opening your arms.*

5 *Then, lower arms down to the level of your bent leg.*

4 *Bend your right knee and raise it higher. Bring your arms back together while turning the palms to face you, holding them vertically.*

6 *Step forward onto right foot and prepare to return to the first standing position.*

OTHER CHANNEL-OPENING THERAPIES

There are several other Eastern therapies based on the theory of *chi* which can help to release the symptoms of stress.

ACUPUNCTURE

Acupuncture is a well-known Chinese remedy for many health problems, and there are now many qualified practitioners in the Western world. The technique consists of releasing the flow of *chi* by placing special needles along specific routes in the body. Keeping the channels open in this way is said to promote and maintain good health. The positions of the needles are identified by the specialist after consultation with the patient about symptoms and medical history. Always make sure that you consult a qualified practitioner because this is obviously not a do-it-yourself therapy. The specialist will ask you questions about your general health, your family's medical history. S/he will also listen to your breathing, and the tone and volume of your voice, and finally will take your pulse. All your answers will give information about the state of your *chi* so that your therapist will be able to determine the number and type of treatments you need to release your flow of *chi*. Acupuncture is often recommended for chronic conditions such as gastro-intestinal problems or inflammation which do not respond to other treatment.

Two types of acupuncture are practiced in the West. Both types originated in China, but one has retained its Eastern characteristics, while the other has developed to suit Western culture and tastes.

◀ *Sometimes your acupuncture therapist will decide to burn herb pellets in the head of the needles. This treatment is said to stimulate the flow of energy and increase the body's power of resistance.*

SHIATSU

Shiatsu, which literally means "finger pressure," is a Japanese therapy which can help to unblock energy channels. The therapy works by putting pressure on specific points to unblock channels so that the *chi* can flow freely. The points, known as acupressure points, are held and pressured for about 3 to 5 seconds. A trained Shiatsu therapist can locate specific pressure points which will help to relieve a variety of complaints such as anxiety, long-term pain, menstrual problems, and insomnia.

Try it for yourself:

✳ To relieve stress and headaches, apply firm pressure to the forehead between the eyebrows.

✳ To alleviate the pain from headaches, massage the temples with a circular motion to stimulate the flow of *chi*.

✳ For general wellbeing, strengthen the *chi* by pressing with the thumb four finger-widths below the navel.

✳ To relieve backache, apply pressure to the middle of the crease behind the knee. Try both knees in turn.

✳ If you are craving a cigarette but trying to give up smoking, apply finger pressure to the area between the two collarbones (make sure you press down on the bone, not on your throat).

✳ If you suffer from insomnia, try squeezing the left ear lobe between thumb and finger. Repeat with the right ear lobe.

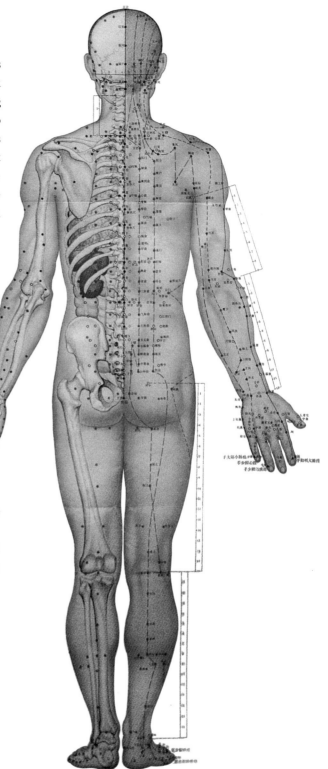

▶ *Your acupuncture therapist will identify your energy channels and determine which need unblocking.*

MORE RELAXATION

We talked about the fundamentals of relaxation during Chapter 1, *Instant Solutions*. This relaxation technique is slightly longer than either of those; it involves deeper relaxation, and you will find that the more you use it, the greater the benefit. Try to incorporate it into your lifestyle twice or three times a week. It is especially beneficial before you start a major task or unpleasant job, because it clears and focuses the mind as well as relaxing the body.

THE TECHNIQUE

You can choose to do this relaxation exercise either sitting or lying down; both of these positions are described in Chapter 1. If you choose the lying-down position, remember to lean forward first and *unpeel* yourself onto the floor. If sitting, make sure your skeleton is supporting your weight, don't let your muscles do the work—they need the rest!

▶ *Follow the steps in their numbered sequence around the body. Take your time so that you can relax fully.*

1 *Close your eyes and … Send your awareness to the thumb on your left hand … and the first finger … the next finger … the next finger … and the little finger, the palm of the hand and the back of the hand. Relax them and let them go.*

2 *Send your awareness to the left lower arm … the left elbow … the upper arm and the left shoulder. Relax them and let them go.*

3 *The left side of the chest … the left side of the waist … the left hip. Relax them and let them go.*

11 *Now send your awareness back to the shoulders, relax them … think into the muscles which run from the shoulders into the neck, up to the head. Relax them and let them go.*

14 *Be aware of the spaces within the body. Now count to three and open your eyes gently. Sit up when you are ready. The world will now seem a better, calmer place.*

12 *Take that relaxation upward, over the muscles of the scalp … and down into the muscles of the face. Unclench the jaw … unclench the teeth … take the tongue as far back as it will go on the roof of the mouth, then let it lie gently in the mouth. Feel the space you have put into the mouth.*

13 *Now put bubbles of space underneath the left eyelid … and all around the left eye socket … and bubbles of space beneath the right eyelid and all around the right eye socket.*

4 *The left upper leg ... the left knee ... the left lower leg and the left ankle. Relax them and let them go.*

5 *The left foot ... the sole of the foot ... the heel ... the toes on the left foot. Relax them and let them go.*

10 *The right foot ... the sole of the foot ... the heel ... the toes on the right foot. Relax them and let them go.*

9 *The right upper leg ... the right knee ... the right lower leg and the right ankle. Relax them and let them go.*

8 *The right side of the chest ... the right side of the waist ... the right hip. Relax them and let them go.*

7 *Send your awareness to the lower arm ... the right elbow ... the upper arm and the right shoulder. Relax them and let them go.*

6 *Now send your awareness to your right hand and repeat as in step 1. Sense the awareness in your thumb, fingers, palm and the back of the hand. Relax them and let them go.*

AUTOGENIC TRAINING

Basic autogenic training uses the same fundamental ideas as the form of progressive relaxation shown here. However, in autogenic training the limbs are treated as a whole: "My arms are heavy. My legs are heavy." Repetitions of these words produce a feeling of calm and relaxation in the body. The repetitions are completed with the statement "I am at peace."

COUNSELING

Sometimes we all need help in solving problems. We may ask friends or family for advice—usually people are only too willing to give it! At times we may take their advice and things still turn out badly for us and we may wonder why. Probably because the advice was what *they* would have done in your situation, but they are not *you*. We are all different, and you cannot always implement someone else's solutions successfully.

HOW COUNSELING WORKS

If you consult a counselor, they will not give you direct advice, but will use strategies to help you find what is the best solution for you as an individual. They will help you to plan a course of action which you can follow, to relieve your stress. They are not judgmental; they are not going to tell you "You should not have done that" or "If you had not done that in the past, you would not be in this mess today."

Choose one who is accredited by a reputable counseling organization—counselors are specially trained to help, and whatever you tell a counselor will be in complete confidence. If a counselor feels that he or she cannot help with your particular problem, you may be referred to another counselor, with your agreement. This is not because you are a difficult person, or because the counselor is inexperienced; it is just that different counselors have different areas of expertise and use different techniques to unlock specific problems.

Some counselors are trained psychotherapists and will try to help the client unlock unconscious thought and memories to resolve problems. Others, such as those who use a form of therapy known as Transactional Analysis, recognize whether we are using the "child," the "parent," or the "adult" within

us, to communicate our wants and needs, depending on our mode of communication. They will help us understand which part of our psyche is operating in a particular situation, and that understanding will enable us to deal better with our responses to the situation.

TRANSACTIONAL ANALYSIS

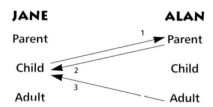

In verbal transactions (conversations) we may use either the parent, child, or adult mode of communication. If the other person responds in the mode in which s/he was addressed, a comfortable transaction results.

For example, if Jane says: "I really don't want to do this task" (transaction 1 above) and Alan replies: "Don't worry, I will help you with it," he is responding in his "parent" mode to his "child" (as in 2 above).

On the other hand, if he replies in "adult" mode (as 3 above): "Don't be silly, just get it done!" they have a crossed transaction and Jane feels uncomfortable and "put down."

▶ *Talking problems through with a counselor helps you to put things in perspective and find your own solutions.*

YOGA

Yoga exercises are designed to keep the body and joints supple. So many of us nowadays lead unnatural, sedentary lives that our joints stiffen prematurely; the postures we adopt when working cause us stiffness and even pain, and the resultant pressures on the nervous system contribute to stress. Yoga exercises can combat this and keep us supple as well as stress-free.

HOW YOGA WORKS

There are various forms of Yoga, all of which originated in India. Yoga is based on the belief that the body has several Chakras, or centers, which control the organs, functions, and spirit of that area. If problems are perceived, the individual focuses on the appropriate Chakra, to alleviate the problems.

Although there are some excellent books on the subject, Yoga is best learned through a class. If you go to a class, you are most likely to be taught Hatha Yoga, which is a series of exercises designed to keep the body supple and sound. It is non-competitive—you do not even have to compete with yourself! You are not expected to think, "I could do that last week, I should be able to do it this week." It is accepted that at different times each one of us is different, therefore we should accept how we are, and not be judgmental about ourselves. Relaxation, too, often forms a part of Yoga teaching.

By focusing into the body during Yoga exercises, you learn to listen to your body, to its wants and needs. The breathing rate and heart rate are slowed during Yoga; in fact, the type of breathing used is

YOGA BREATHING TECHNIQUE
1 *Sit in the Lotus Pose or any comfortable seated position to "center-in," or exclude the outside world.*

2 *Close the right nostril with your thumb. Breathe in to a count of four, keeping the right nostril closed. Retain the breath for a count of four.*

3 *Remove your thumb and breathe out to a count of eight. Repeat several times, closing the left and right nostril alternately.*

important and is incorporated into each exercise. Here are the beginnings of control of the autonomic responses, which are usually assumed to be beyond our control. Practiced Yogics are famous for existing with only small amounts of air and other feats that would leave the rest of us literally gasping. You may not want to achieve such abilities, but a feeling of control over your responses is useful when trying to manage stress, or achieve a healthy lifestyle in today's hectic world.

► *The Lotus Pose, which is favored for "centering in" and excluding the outside world. If you cannot manage this, choose a seated posture which you find comfortable.*

AROMATHERAPY

Aromatherapy—a form of massage using special scented oils—uses the link between our sense of smell and the brain to change our mood state. The influence of scents on the body has been known for thousands of years. For example, pots of scented ointments were found in the Egyptian tombs. The basis of modern aromatherapy began in France, in the late 1920s, when the healing properties of lavender oil were described in a scientific paper.

THE OILS

If you go to a trained aromatherapist, you will be given a body massage using a mixture of essential oils specially made up for you, blended in a carrier oil. Very few essential oils may be applied directly to the skin, so they should always be combined with a carrier oil first.

You can give yourself a similar treatment at home, or you can use a few drops of oil in the bath for the desired effect. Some essential oils are relaxing, while others are invigorating. They are all subject to personal preferences, so choose the ones which appeal to you—these will do the most good. You may find that a mixture is most effective, but never mix more than three oils together.

Real essential oils are very expensive, and are generally used for body massage. You only need to use a few drops, however, mixed with a carrier to achieve the desired effect, whether this be relaxing, calming, invigorating, or whatever result the oil is designed to achieve. Cheaper oils (also often called "essential oils," which is confusing) are useful for baths or to use in an oilburner. Electric or candle burners will diffuse the aroma throughout the room.

CHOOSING THE RIGHT OIL

✳ **To aid relaxation** Calendula, chamomile, clary sage, jasmine, lavender, marjoram, patchouli, rose, rosewood, sandalwood, valerian, ylang-ylang

✳ **To uplift the spirits** Basil, bergamot, geranium, juniper, lavender

✳ **To aid sleeping** Benzoin, clary sage, patchouli, rose, ylang-ylang

✳ **To reduce stress** Chamomile, geranium, lavender, marjoram, peppermint, sandalwood

A NOTE OF CAUTION
Some of these oils are very strong; if you are pregnant or suffer from epilepsy, consult an aromatherapist before using them.

▼ *Lightly massage carefully selected and blended oils into your skin to lift your mood.*

▶ *Scented candles, oil burners, and essential oils exert a powerful chemical action in the body which works to change your mood.*

HEALTHY EATING

Under stress your digestive system slows down. You may not feel like eating at all, or you may simply nibble at food, especially sweet things, the so-called "comfort foods," such as chocolate. Scientists believe that these may bring some comfort because their components act directly on the brain, but this effect is short-lived, and they provide little or no nourishment.

KEEPING UP YOUR STRENGTH

Stress depletes the body's resources, so it is essential to eat properly to replenish these resources. As the digestive system will not be working properly when you are under stress, a number of smaller meals throughout the day will be more beneficial than one big meal in the evening. Also, some foods are more nourishing than others; as a general rule, processed foods are the least nourishing. As to vegetarianism, the choice is your own. Humans have been eating meat for thousands of years, so there seems little to indicate that it should be excluded from our diets, except on moral grounds or for specific medical reasons such as allergies.

▶ *Try this diet to help reduce your stress levels: eat plenty of oily fish, fruits, and vegetables, whole wheat bread, and other cereals which are high in fiber but low in fat.*

HEALTHY EATING PLAN

A normal, balanced diet would include:

✳ **For vitamins and minerals** Fresh fruits and vegetables, rich in anti-oxidants which are essential for good health

✳ **For carbohydrates (to keep up energy levels)** Pasta, bread (especially whole wheat), potatoes, rice, and cereals

✳ **For protein** Fish (especially oily fish such as mackerel and herrings which are rich in Omega 3 fatty acids and identified as preventatives in coronary heart disease and the treatment of arthritis), nuts, soya, and chicken. Red meats, eggs, and cheese, but eaten sparingly

Foods to avoid or limit include:

✳ **Fatty foods**, such as cream, butter, mayonnaise, and rich sauces

✳ **Sugar** and **salt**, which may disrupt the body's chemical balance

✳ **Caffeine**—a limited amount (3 cups) is fine as it "keeps you going." There is caffeine in tea, coffee, cocoa, cola, and many other soft drinks

A stressbusting diet would include:

✳ Leafy green vegetables
✳ Citrus fruits
✳ Bananas
✳ Whole wheat bread
✳ Cereal (oats are particularly good)
✳ Mackerel or herrings

Take time to enjoy your food; eat it with love, and in company if possible. A meal hastily snatched does little for either body or spirit.

HYPNOTHERAPY

For many people, the word "hypnosis" conjures up an image of stage hypnotists, who often make fools of their subjects for the entertainment of others. A hypnotherapist does no such thing and will only work for the good of those who attend sessions. Make sure your hypnotherapist is a member of a professional body, and you need have no qualms.

HOW HYPNOTHERAPY WORKS

When you attend your first session, the hypnotherapist will discuss with you what you wish to achieve, whether simply to feel more relaxed, or more comfortable in social environments, to reduce phobic fears, or give up smoking—hypnosis can assist with a number of problems such as these. You will then be shown how to relax, and a trance state induced. This is not total unconsciousness, more like very deep relaxation; at no time during hypnotism could you be persuaded to do something that was completely out of character, for example, to harm someone, or give all your money away! This is why the therapist needs to be sure at the outset that you really *are* committed to giving up smoking, or whatever.

Depending on the type of result you wish to achieve, one or more sessions may be necessary; sometimes a therapist will provide a tape for you to practice with at home. More and more clients are affirming how helpful hypnotherapy has been in helping them with specific and previously unassailable problems, such as quitting smoking.

Where hypnotherapy is used in the practice of psychotherapy, the subconscious can also be explored, and long-forgotten experiences may be uncovered. This needs to be undertaken only with a fully experienced psychotherapist, as these memories may be painful and the individual concerned may need further expert help. For the vast majority of people this is not a necessary experience.

The route that hypnosis takes is to bypass the conscious mind, to the subconscious, where suggestions may be planted more easily, and which will retain their influence even when the conscious mind takes over again.

SELF-HYPNOSIS

It is perfectly possible to undertake self-hypnosis; there are a number of tapes which you can purchase, to suit whatever purpose you have in mind, which can be used quite safely. Induce a state of relaxation in yourself, as directed in one of the sections on relaxation in this book, and when you are comfortable and relaxed, switch on your tape or CD. When the tape or CD has finished, there are key words to return you to a normal level of consciousness, and you will find yourself feeling pleasantly relaxed and at peace.

◄ *Many hypnotherapists provide tapes for their clients which they may use at home. Alternatively, you can buy self-hypnosis tapes and CDs to help you quit smoking, induce relaxation, regain confidence, and other common aims in hypnotherapy.*

REPLACING IRRATIONAL THOUGHTS

Often, it is our own irrational thoughts that provide barriers to solving problems. Such thoughts may pop, unbidden, into our heads, when anything new, which could *potentially* be a problem, or be seen as stressful, comes along. You need to examine these irrational thoughts, find out why they are occurring, and replace them with rational, logical thoughts, which will in themselves reduce stress.

EXAMINING YOUR THOUGHTS

The next time a new task is proposed and you begin to feel stressed, challenge yourself as to why; stop and examine your actual thoughts. Your own thoughts may be self-defeating or anxiety-provoking, so that the stress you feel is actually coming from within yourself, not from any external pressures. If someone else told you these were their thoughts, what would you suggest to them? Be your own best friend, and suggest a logical way to look at the problem.

For various reasons we often already have a set of irrational beliefs, frequently consisting of black-and-white statements, for example:

Jill: I *must* be successful.
Anne: I *must* get a promotion or I shall be a *total failure*.
Mark: I did that wrong, it just shows I am *totally useless*.

Each of these statements can be challenged.

There is nothing on earth to say that Jill must be successful; if she isn't, life will still go on—nations will not fall just because she is unsuccessful. She may prefer success, but it is not obligatory, so she needs to put things in perspective.

Anne states that she must get a promotion or be a total failure, but there is no rational reason why failure to gain one promotion should blight the rest of her life.

In the same way, the fact that Mark has done one thing wrong does not mean that he is totally useless; it is certain that in his lifetime he has done many other things *right*.

People like Jill, Anne, and Mark are imposing stress on themselves by producing these extreme statements and beliefs about themselves, that have no real foundation. By challenging these statements and reducing them to more reasonable ideas—for example, "I would like this promotion, if possible"—they can reduce their stress.

◄ *Sometimes we can feel as if our whole world will tumble down around us. Irrational thoughts are thoughts without foundation. Replace them with positive, rational thoughts about your needs and capabilities, and you will find your stress levels will decrease considerably.*

NEGATIVE THOUGHTS CHECKLIST

Are any of these ways of thinking familiar to you?

Must statements You criticize yourself or others using words such as "should," "must," "ought to," "have to." Beware of such words; they reveal the inner tyrant in you—what Transactional Analysts call the "parent."

Black-and-white thinking Everything is going to be either catastrophic or wonderful. Real life is usually somewhere between the two.

Negative thoughts You discount all the positives about yourself, counting only the negatives. Or, one negative event is viewed as a neverending pattern of defeat.

If you have such patterns of thinking, be aware of them; challenge your thought processes and be more positive about yourself. A few mistakes do not label you as a loser for life. Someone who has never made a mistake has never actually attempted anything!

MORE EXERCISE

People who take in an inadequate supply of oxygen may be starving the brain of its essential supply, so it is no wonder they cannot think clearly or constantly feel "down" mentally. This is where aerobic exercise can help, for it increases the heart-rate and provokes the lungs to take in extra oxygen. The oxygen is passed into the bloodstream and transported efficiently around the body, due to the increased heart-rate. Some of it, of course, enters the brain's circulatory system. The brain cannot function without this supply of oxygen, and there are times when we all need extra oxygen.

WHERE TO EXERCISE

There are a number of aerobics classes which you could attend. The better classes will give you a fitness assessment first, and many impose an upper-age limit for complete beginners. Let the instructor know if you have any health problems, such as high blood pressure. You will need proper shoes, in order not to injure your feet, legs, or ankles.

There are also some very good videos of aerobic exercises which you can use at home, with the advantage that you can stop when you personally have done enough, without feeling that you have to keep up with the rest of the class. (If you are over 50, be extra careful if you do not normally take exercise; it may be better for you to consult a doctor first, or have an assessment at a gym.)

A GENTLE INTRODUCTION

As a gradual approach to the idea of aerobics and to make sure that your body and your mind are on the alert, try this exercise—gently at first, especially if you are not used to exercising.

1 *Stand with your feet wide apart and your arms above your head.*

2 *From the main position, with feet wide apart and arms above your head, bend gently to the right.*

▼ *Swaying Grass*
For improving the flexibility of the upper body, and improving the breathing.

3 *Now bend gently to the left. Return to the main position and repeat the movements ten times.*

Now try the following exercise that is good for clearing the head, giving a sense of "readiness" and purpose, and casting off stress. It is sometimes called "The Strengthener."

1 Stand with your feet apart, and on an in-breath, raise your arms diagonally in the air.

2 Now breathe out in a long, slow breath, bringing your arms down so that your fingers meet at the navel, with your elbows bent. At the same time, bend your knees slightly, keeping your feet flat on the floor and your spine straight.

3 Breathe in deeply, raising your arms back above the head to position 1, but keeping your knees bent. Pause.

4 Breathe out in a long, slow breath, bringing your arms down so your fingers again meet at the navel, keeping the knees bent.

5 Repeat steps 3 and 4 two more times.

6 Finally, breathe in deeply, raising your arms above your head diagonally and straightening your legs. Then breathe out slowly, allowing your arms to fall gently to your sides. Relax your legs (in turn) by rolling each foot onto the ball of the foot, bending the knee and ankle joints. Do this several times for each leg.

You may find this exercise is hard on your leg muscles the first time you try, but you will gradually strengthen them and soon find it much easier.

VISUALIZATION

Visualization is a powerful technique, utilized in many programs, such as Neuro-Linguistic Programming (NLP), for example. It involves visualizing yourself in a different dimension, of time, or space, or place. It is very useful if you have a specific problem, or two alternatives you cannot choose between. You can visualize yourself in both positions and decide where you are most comfortable before you commit yourself in front of others.

GETTING STARTED

Visualization involves using the imagination and visual imagery (in some cases with the eyes shut), which makes it difficult for some people who would not describe their visual sense as of greatest importance to them. As with a number of techniques, practice makes perfect. Read the following exercises first, then try to do the visualizations with your eyes closed.

A place of relaxation Visualize a large T.V. screen; on it is a beautiful landscape or seascape which you find relaxing—a beach, perhaps, or rolling hills, or a country lane. Feel the warmth of a summer's day around you, and smell the aromas associated with that scene. Hear the sounds there: the waves lapping on the beach, or the sounds of the birds. Feel yourself as part of that scene, and step inside it. Reach out and touch the objects there—a leaf or grass, or the sand trickling through your fingers at the beach. Stay in your visualization for a while until you choose to return. On re-entry into reality, you will feel calmer and happier.

The relaxed "you" When you feel tense or stressed, visualize yourself like that, on the left of a T.V. screen, featuring large. Now, in the background, smaller and to the right, picture yourself as you would like to be, perhaps calm, self-assured, worry-free, confident, self-possessed, and "in charge." You may need to recall a time in your past when you felt like that, in order to make the image realistic to yourself. Gradually make this "confident self" image larger and superimpose it on the "worried" image;

once it is in place, hold it there. Remember how you felt, to be worry-free, remember any sounds, feelings, aromas, or feelings of touch associated with it. Then gradually return to the real world, bringing that image of yourself with you, and stay with it.

The time line You may be faced with making a choice in the very near future; you have weighed up the pros and cons and still cannot come to a decision. The uncertainty is causing you to feel stressed, and the possibility of making and implementing the wrong choice is creating even more stress. Perhaps you have the opportunity to apply for advancement at work, for example. The new position would enhance your standing and self-esteem,

and the extra money would be useful, but you would have more responsibility and longer hours, and would possibly see less of your family. How can you resolve this?

Draw an imaginary line across the middle of the room, or lay a tape measure across it. Stand well to one side of the line: this is where you are now, at this moment in time. Close your eyes and visualize your life as it is—your home and family, the pleasures and responsibilities associated with them as they are; your work, colleagues, and workload, your good days and bad; your social life, friends, outings, and close circle of acquaintances. How do you feel? Happy, content, bored, restless?

Now open your eyes, walk deliberately across the line, and turn to face the place you have come from. Close your eyes again. Visualize yourself in the new position: you have been given advancement at work. Imagine the new work situation, its challenges, rewards, and responsibilities. Imagine any changes in your home situation, perhaps less time, but more money—perhaps better vacations. Visualize the changes which might occur in your social life, and weigh these up.

Open your eyes and decide which side of the line you want to be on. Be happy in your choice!

◀ *Visualize separating yourself from the present and finding yourself in a place you would like to be, where you can relax and be yourself with confidence.*

OSTEOPATHY

"What's osteopathy got to do with stress—it's about manipulating bones?" some of you may exclaim. It is true that the practice of osteopathy is concerned with manipulating and repositioning parts of the skeletal system which have become out of proper alignment, through trauma, injury, or bad posture. Those are exactly the reasons osteopathy is included in a book on stress.

THE EFFECTS OF TRAUMA AND INJURY

Trauma and injury not only produce physical problems, but they also provoke stress in the individual affected. Think back to a time when you yourself have suffered physical injury, such as back injury. I am sure you will agree that you also suffered psychological stress at the same time, for a number of reasons. Maybe you were suffering with pain, or frustrated because you could not get around as well as usual, or anxious because there were jobs you needed to attend to, but could not.

Stress is undoubtedly a result of trauma or injury. Bad posture can, in fact, be caused by stress. When we are stressed, we hold ourselves tensely. We are stiff, we often poke our chins forward, and we move awkwardly (this sometimes leads to injury!). If bad posture continues for some time, we may bring skeletal injury upon ourselves.

VISITING AN OSTEOPATH

Always select an osteopath who is a member of the appropriate professional body, to ensure that he or she has received full training, and is covered by full professional insurance.

▼ *Backache is one of the commonest complaints and reasons for missing work. It is often caused by muscle tension brought on by stress.*

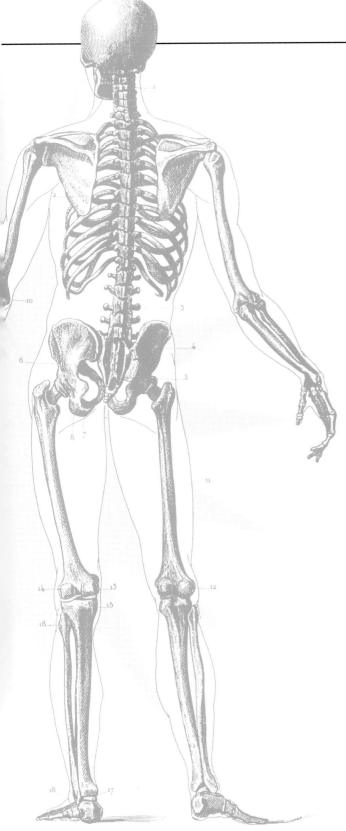

On your first visit your osteopath will take some time looking into your general health and past history, as well as the reason for your current visit.

He or she will then give you a physical assessment and tell you approximately how many visits you will need, over what period of time, and what sort of progress you can expect.

A good osteopath will detect and advise on poor posture. Injuries and misalignments can be corrected through manipulation. Nerves which are trapped or, which through misalignment are not lying in their appropriate position, may be sending aberrant messages to the brain; these may be received as cries of distress, thereby causing the perception of stress.

The manipulation process necessarily involves massage, which is in itself stress-relieving, but even more stress reduction is experienced from the ensuing pain relief. Some of the techniques used may involve some discomfort; it is for you to decide whether the end product was worth the discomfort.

◀ *The vertebrae of the back comprise a number of small bones placed one above the other. Any slight misalignment of these small bones can cause severe discomfort. Back pain can be relieved by manipulation by an osteopath.*

MEDITATION

This technique originated in the East, but has found great acceptance in the West. Meditation does not have to be related to one of the Eastern religions: it is simply a clearing and focusing of the mind. This shuts out all other stimuli and clears away the mind's "clutter."

A RESTFUL MIND

During meditation a number of physiological changes take place: the blood pressure and heart-rate drop, the breathing rate slows down, and the brainwaves of the cortex show the "alpha" rhythm, which typifies the wakeful yet resting state of the body. This rhythm would change, if you dropped off to sleep, into one of the "sleep patterns"—meditation is not a kind of sleep, but a deeply focused yet resting state of mind.

HOW TO MEDITATE

Meditation is usually carried out in a seated position. If you cannot sit comfortably in the favored Lotus Pose, don't worry—choose any position which is similar but comfortable. Prop your back against a wall, if you like, or place cushions under your knees; you cannot meditate effectively and rise to higher thoughts if your mind keeps returning to the fact that your body is uncomfortable. In fact, when you first try to practice meditation, your mind will try all sorts of tricks to stop you from focusing: it will remind you of jobs you have not done, people you need to see, and so on. Your mind is not used to clearing and concentrating on just one item.

The focus of your meditation is up to you. Some people choose to sit in front of a candle and focus on its flame; others repeat a mantra, or a simple word of their own choice. You may prefer something meaningful, such as the word "relax," or you could try saying aloud "OM" with a long-drawn out-breath, which originates from Eastern meditation. Its resonance, when said aloud, is said to have an effect upon the body. Or repeat "one" on the out-breath, as suggested for *Quick Relaxation* on page 14.

FOUR-POINT PLAN FOR EFFECTIVE MEDITATION

* Meditation is a technique which comes with practice. It cannot be done in a hurry, so choose a time when you will not be interrupted.
* Promise yourself you will practice every day for a week. Choose a set time and place and stick to it.
* Set a realistic period of time for your meditation, and stick to that, even if it does not seem to be working.
* As other thoughts intrude into your mind (and they will!), imagine enclosing them in a bubble and blowing them away.

◀ *You can meditate in any position as long as it is comfortable. Experiment with different positions—you may find that sitting cross-legged works best for you.*

► *A candle flame is often used as the focus for meditation. In the background is the "OM" symbol. The long lower curve represents the dream state; the upper curve represents the waking state, and the curve issuing from the center symbolizes deep, dreamless sleep. The crescent shape represents the veil of illusion and the dot, the transcendental state. When the meditator's spirit passes through the veil and rests in the transcendental, s/he is liberated from all three of the lower states and their attributes.*

HERBALISM AND HOMEOPATHY

These two therapies—one ancient and the other only a couple of hundred years old—can provide an effective alternative to the orthodox drugs prescribed to alleviate stress symptoms.

RELAXING REMEDIES

Chamomile	Usually taken as a drink
Evening primrose	Recommended particularly for pre-menstrual tension; also for arthritis and high cholesterol (both of which are also thought to be related to stress)
Hops	Can be infused as a drink, or used in a "hops pillow" to induce sleep
Rescue Remedy	A mixture of rose, cherry blossom, Star of Bethlehem, impatiens, and clematis, it was discovered by Dr. Edward Bach, a homeopathic physician; it provides prompt relief from psychological and physical trauma
Skullcap	A very strong relaxant
Tarragon	A teaspoonful, steeped in 2 pints of hot water for half an hour, is a remedy for insomnia and tension
Valerian	A very strong relaxant, so do not take too much. Do not try to prepare this from the plant itself: it can be poisonous unless prepared properly
Wood betony	For stress-induced headaches

HERBALISM

Some of the best-known drugs we use today have their origins in plants; aspirin can be synthesized from willow bark, digitalis comes from foxgloves, and there are many others. Yet for many years in Western civilizations, herbalists were regarded with suspicion, and thought of as "cranks," whereas in some Eastern countries, herbalism is taught as part of the curriculum in medical schools.

Fortunately, Western society has begun to accept that orthodox medicine and herbal remedies can co-exist, even complementing each other. On investigation, many of the well-known herbal remedies were found to have a chemical basis which acted in a particular way on the biochemistry of the body—similar to synthetic drugs, but in a more natural way. When taken for stress, chemical tranquilizers often seem like sledgehammers, whereas a herbal remedy will provide a more gentle, gradual effect. Health food stores and an increasing number of pharmacies stock and will advise on suitable herbal remedies, for a number of conditions.

HOMEOPATHY

Homeopathic medicine was developed by Samuel Hahnemann (1755–1843), a German physician. It works on the principle that if the body's own defenses can be mobilized, they will provide a more effective cure. Consequently homeopathic medicines are not designed as "cures," but as a means to sensitize the body to produce its own cure. Each remedy also suits a different type of person, so treatment needs to be prescribed by a qualified homeopath, who will need to know many details before prescribing a remedy. Many of the medicines have herbal origins; they are diluted many, many times, until there is only a

whisper of the active ingredient left. Yet numerous studies have shown that homeopathic remedies are effective, whereas taking a *placebo* (a pill which has no active ingredient) is not, demonstrating that it is not simply the expectation of getting better which is at the basis of the homeopathic success.

▼ *Medicines derived from herbs are currently enjoying a resurgence in popularity; many clinical trials have demonstrated the effectiveness of these natural remedies.*

MANAGING YOUR TIME EFFECTIVELY

If you are simply trying to pack 25 hours into a 24-hour day, time management cannot help you: you must cut down your workload. If, on the other hand, you feel you could be making better use of your time, this is just what time management can do.

ANALYZING YOUR DAY

First you need to analyze your workload; write down all the tasks you do in a day, and how long you are likely to spend on each of them. It is also very useful to confirm this by filling in a time log of how you have spent your time on a typical day. From this you will be able to:

* organize your workload in a sensible order
* see which tasks you can delegate to other people
* identify where and when you are indulging in time-wasting activities

Time-wasting activities may include items such as making numerous cups of tea or coffee, which you don't really need (and these frequently have to be followed by numerous trips to the toilet, another time-wasting activity!). Simply chatting with people, even those you don't really want to talk to, consumes a great deal of time and could probably be cut back, unless it is an activity you enjoy so much you count it as a hobby or a stress-reducing activity! You need to strike a balance here: which is the least stressful—cutting down the "chatting" time or being short of time at the end of the day? Only you can choose.

Completing paperwork is a task which needs to be incorporated into your time, whether it is paperwork in conjunction with your job, or the household accounts, paying bills, or filling in forms. Yes, it may be boring, but if it is not done regularly, it tends to pile up and then it does become stressful.

DELEGATING

Many of us are bad at delegating tasks to others. Maybe we think other people cannot do things as well as we can; this may be a wrong assumption, so try them and see. They may do them differently but not worse. Perhaps you think you should not give others tasks which you could do; wrong again! Delegation at work is part

satisfying crossing things off when the task is done. It is also less stressful for you if you have a list, because once items are written down, you don't have to worry about forgetting them. Trying to remember all the day's jobs without a written list takes up brain-time which could be better employed in "doing."

Once items are written on a list, you can see at a glance which should take priority, and which job can logically follow another. For example, if there are two calls to make in close areas, combine the journey; it saves backtracking later.

The benefits of improved time management include:

✳ getting more tasks done
✳ feeling "in control" of your time
✳ not constantly feeling rushed or tired
✳ increased free time
✳ less stress

of good management; delegation at home is character-building. It is good for your son or daughter to have the responsibility of a regular task: walking the dog, unloading the dishwasher, vacuuming the living-room as well as their bedroom. If you have more than one job available which is within their capabilities, you can offer them a choice.

GETTING ORGANIZED

Diaries and wallcharts are essentials for making sure you do not forget things. Make sure you consult them at the start of each day. At home, try one of the "day-to-a-page" diaries; leave it in the kitchen for all the family to enter where they are going and what they are doing. That way, children realize that they cannot all be picked up from different places at the same time, and means that no one is forgotten.

Make lists! Not just shopping lists, but "things to do today" or "this week" lists. It is very

◀ *If you use your time more efficiently, you will have more time available for leisure activities and enjoyment of the things you want to do.*

GIVE YOUR LIFE SOME DIRECTION

We can all feel as if time and events are controlling us rather than us controlling them. This can lead to us feeling stressed and sometimes disappointed with ourselves that we have let our lives be so busy, yet in reality we are drifting without aim.

Setting goals and aims It can be enlightening for us to set out our real goals and aims in life and put them in order. Think about what you would like to achieve in either your career or private life over the next year and next five or ten years. Write your ideas down, in order, in two columns.

Evaluating your progress Develop a realistic action plan and time-scale to acheive these goals. Monitor your progress regularly, perhaps every month to remind you what you are working towards.

CHAPTER 5

A CHANGE OF LIFESTYLE

Sometimes we not only need to change external circumstances to reduce our stress levels, but we also need to change  ourselves. We are our own worst enemies at times, when we produce stress for ourselves, by our actions, thoughts, and behaviors. These we need to change. Stress management is not just something you learn, use once, and throw away. In order to be effective, we need to incorporate stress management into our lives; frequently this means we have to make changes in our

 lifestyle. These changes are all to the good: they will make us feel better, happier, and healthier.

A HEALTHIER LIFESTYLE

By adopting a healthy lifestyle we can buffer the effects of stress. Main areas for change include diet, exercise, and relaxation. Changes which you need to make can be incorporated into your life, little by little. It is far less stressful to plan for change rather than try to change overnight. With a little thought, changes can often be incorporated into your daily routine.

Diet It is better to eat three moderate meals a day, rather than one large meal. Meals should include plenty of fresh fruit and vegetables; try taking fruit instead of a pudding. Fill up with fiber-rich foods, such as whole wheat bread, pasta, and potatoes cooked in their skins. Leafy green vegetables are a good source of vitamins and minerals. Choose low-fat foods, low-fat or skim milk, and polyunsaturated fats. Be sparing with salt, which tends to raise blood pressure.

Drink plenty of water. A moderate amount of alcohol (one or two units a day) will do no harm, and some scientists suggest it does good in moderation. The same can be said of caffeine. Be cautious about large quantities of low-calorie drinks; some of the sugar substitutes may affect some people, making them hyperactive—a bad combination with stress.

▶ *Include some exercise into your lifestyle; choose something you will enjoy and continue.*

Exercise If you have not taken regular exercise for years, start slowly and build up gradually. Try to build some form of exercise into your daily routine. For example, try parking the car some distance away from your workplace, then briskly walk the remainder of the journey (remember, you will also have to walk back in the evening). If you travel to work by bus, get off a stop early and walk the rest of the way. Use the stairs, rather than the elevator. Remember, exercise may leave you breathless, but should not leave you gasping and speechless.

Carry out some form of noncompetitive exercise for 15 minutes two or three times a week; swimming, bicycling, and hill-walking are all ideal. Try to make sure at least some of your exercise is carried out in the fresh, clean air. Do not begin exercise for an hour after meals—your body is busy digesting, so don't ask it to do two things at once! If you decide to take up a new form of exercise after reading this book, start slowly, and don't do too much to begin with. If you are over 35, or have had any recent health problems, check with your doctor before taking up a strenuous sport.

Relaxation and leisure However busy your life, make sure you keep some time for leisure activities, hobbies, or whatever you find relaxing and enjoyable. Make sure your weekends are not the same as your weekdays; we all need a change. Especially allow time to have the sleep you need.

CRISIS CONTROL

Many life stresses are minor, but even these should not be underestimated. When they accumulate, as often they do, their pressure is considerable, and this is why we need to know techniques for stress management. However, when a crisis occurs, the impact is huge and immediate, different from the insidious onset of numerous smaller stresses.

What constitutes a crisis? Obviously you will know a crisis when it hits you, but as examples I would suggest such events as bereavement, arrest, a serious illness or accident in the family or affecting yourself, sudden loss of your job or dismissal, or major environmental trauma such as flood, earthquake, or fire. The stress resulting from any of these will be immediate and extreme.

Staying calm This is easier to say than to do, but it is important to try. Remember your breathing, and concentrate on the out-breath to take tension away from the body. Do what is within your power to do in the first instance, and then call expert help. The biggest mistake people make in a crisis is that they try to cope alone. It is not a sign of weakness to call for help; that is what the expert agencies are there for. If you feel that you need spiritual rather than practical help, seek it from friends, counselors, or religious leaders. Spiritual or emotional support is just as necessary in a crisis as is practical expert assistance. You need to share your experience with others, to gain encouragement and sympathy from them so that you can keep going.

If you don't know where to turn for advice, try the telephone directory. There are a number of agencies listed under "counseling" in most cities. For practical help, doctors, lawyers, or other professionals can usually suggest where you can get the most appropriate form of assistance.

▶ *A crisis or traumatic situation is always easier to bear if it is shared with someone else.*

APPRECIATING LIFE MORE

Become more aware of what goes on in your life; learn to plan in advance for stressful periods and events, so that you weather them more easily. Look at your life objectively and identify your major sources of stress; develop plans to eliminate them or deal with them. Make constructive stress-management strategies part of your life, and you will become more resilient. If you are forward-planning and not constantly overwhelmed by stress, you will begin to appreciate life more—you will have time and energy to see the flowers along the way.

Develop your thinking skills Cultivate positive thoughts and try to eliminate negative thoughts. Try to give away at least one positive affirmation per day, either to yourself or to someone else (make sure you do not neglect yourself). Don't assume that others are thinking badly of you and what you do; jumping to conclusions is a fruitless exercise. Challenge thoughts which contain the words "must," "should," and

▶ *Allowing time for rest, relaxation and leisure pursuits makes you appreciate life more.*

"ought to" ("I must do this," "He should do that"); ask yourself, "why?" There are few actions which are compulsory; there are nearly always options. Leave the options open, for yourself as well as others.

Allow yourself to have feelings Don't suppress your feelings and emotions; we are humans, not automatons, and emotions are a natural part of our make-up. Learn to acknowledge your own feelings, and when appropriate, to share them with other people. Be able to say "I am angry," "I am sad," "I love you," to others. Emotions need to be expressed, not bottled up and turned inward. Grief, particularly, needs to be expressed in order to be dealt with effectively. If you are worried or anxious, take your anxieties to the person who has caused them, or to someone who can allay them; do not keep them to yourself. Learn to be flexible and adaptable, so that feelings and emotions will be experienced as less frightening and not so extreme.

Develop effective behaviors Learn to say no. Be assertive, but not aggressive, to make sure that you are not "put upon." Avoid blaming others for situations which arise, but do not take the blame yourself for something that was not of your making. If you acknowledge problems as soon as they appear, you can begin to deal with them effectively—or, at least make plans to minimize their effect. If you deny that problems are arising, they simply get bigger and more complex.

Learn to manage your time effectively. Find things which you can cut out of your day, by delegating them or simply not doing them any longer. A little organization may take time initially, but will save far more time in the long run, and life will run more smoothly.

A ZEST FOR LIVING

There are various ways you can improve your enthusiasm for life. A more positive outlook in general will help you cope with stressful situations and will give you a better sense of perspective.

Your lifestyle Develop a lifestyle that will strengthen you against stress: a healthy diet, relaxation, exercise, leisure activities you enjoy, are all components that will enrich your life. Choose how you spend your free time; if you don't want to spend it in doing things for other people, then do your own thing. It is *your* life, and *your* choice. Maintain your sense of humor; many situations have a funny side. If you can laugh about your situation, it will help to lift your mood and make you feel better.

Make sure that you keep some time aside for yourself each day, to be on your own to practice your chosen form of relaxation, or to listen to music, or just to listen to your own thoughts, to keep in touch with yourself. Have the courage to change the things you can change and the wisdom not to attempt to change the impossible.

Networking Spend time with the people you really want to be with, and with those you want to be like. If you are a Type-A personality, try not to spend time with other Type-As, and if you have to, try not to compete with them. Spend time with positive, happy people, and avoid the negative, depressing ones. Avoid having depressing conversations. If you are under stress yourself, don't let other people load their stress on to you. Stress is catching; recent research has shown that a husband's stress affects his wife, and vice versa. The same is almost certainly true of friends and work colleagues.

Establish and maintain networks of friends and relatives, made up of people you really want to include; tell them you value their friendship. Be able to ask for direct help when you need it, and be ready to accept when it is offered voluntarily.

Spiritual development Maintain a strong belief in your own personal values; if you are convinced in your heart that something is right, you can act more decisively. Stress is reduced if you act in accordance with your beliefs and values. Establish a sense of purpose and direction to your life; smaller events will fall into place along the way. Learn to transcend stressful situations; maintain a sense of proportion and view any stress in the grand scheme of things. That way, its seeming importance is diminished so you can deal with it. By focusing your attention, you are reducing your stress and also finding the most efficient way of functioning.

▶ *Developing a healthy lifestyle and a positive outlook on life will give you a new zest for living, whatever your age.*

GLOSSARY

ACTH—adrenocorticotrophic hormone, which is released by the pituitary and prompts the adrenal glands to release glucocorticoids, for example cortisol

ACUPUNCTURE—a Chinese therapy which uses needles to release the flow of *chi* along its channels

ADRENALINE—a hormone released by the adrenal glands which speeds up heart rate. It also acts as a chemical in the brain during the transmission of nerve messages.

ANS—Autonomic Nervous System—that part of the body's nervous system which automatically regulates body functions such as digestion, blood pressure, and heart-rate.

AROMATHERAPY—the use of scents to stimulate mood changes through the sense of smell

CHD—cardiac heart disease; health problems associated with the heart and/or blood vessels to and from the heart

CNS—Central Nervous System includes the brain, which computes perceptions, solves problems and gives instructions, and the spinal cord, which controls reflexes

COGNITIVE BEHAVIOR THERAPY—a therapy which involves conscious thought processes (cognitions) in order to change unwanted behaviors

CORTISOL—released by the adrenal glands, cortisol raises blood pressure and increases metabolic rate

COUNSELING—a one-to-one discussion of an individual's problems, where s/he is assisted in finding solutions

ENDOCRINE SYSTEM—the system of hormones which interacts and brings about chemical changes in the body

ENDORPHINS—chemicals which are mainly active in the brain, changing and uplifting mood state; sometimes called "the body's own morphine"

HOMEOPATHY—a form of treatment which works by sensitizing the body to produce its own defenses and cure

HORMONES—chemicals which are produced by glands for a specific purpose; for example insulin, produced by the pancreas, to deal with sugar in the body

HYPNOTHERAPY—a therapy to bring about changes in the state of conscious awareness, by the use of suggestions made under hypnosis

IMMUNE SYSTEM—a system of fighter cells made primarily in the bone marrow and thymus gland to combat disease or bacteria attacking the body. These cells circulate in the blood and lymph fluid

MEDITATION—focusing on the inner self and excluding all external stimuli and distractions; this is another changed state of consciousness

PSYCHOTHERAPY—a one-to-one, in-depth examination of unconscious processes which may be exerting an undersirable effect on the individual

RATIONAL-EMOTIVE BEHAVIOR THERAPY—a therapy which aims to uncover irrational thoughts and emotions and to rationalize these in order to regulate behavior

REFLEXOLOGY—areas of the body are "mapped" on the feet. By massaging the feet, body areas are stimulated

RELAXATION—the process of de-stressing the mind while reducing tension in the muscles of the body

SHIATSU—a Japanese channel-opening therapy, which utilizes pressure on specific points of the body, to release the flow of energy

T'AI CHI—a series of exercises and movements which also serve to focus the mind and promote self-awareness (mindfulness)

TYPE-A—a type of personality identified as being highly competitive, aggressive and won't "let up"; thought to be high risk for CHD

YOGA—there are many forms of Yoga; in the Western world you are more likely to encounter Hatha Yoga, a combination of stretching exercises, controlled breathing, and relaxation

INDEX

CREDITS

Quarto would like to acknowledge and thank the
following for providing pictures used in this book.

Image Bank p. 6, p. 8(br), p. 18, p. 19, p. 28,
p. 29, p. 70, p. 71, p. 101, p. 103, p. 105, p. 107.
Pictor p. 75.

All other photographs are the copyright of
Quarto Publishing plc.

**This book is dedicated to Eileen, my Yoga
teacher, for all her help.**